Form 178 rev. 11-00

Materials Science
GLASS

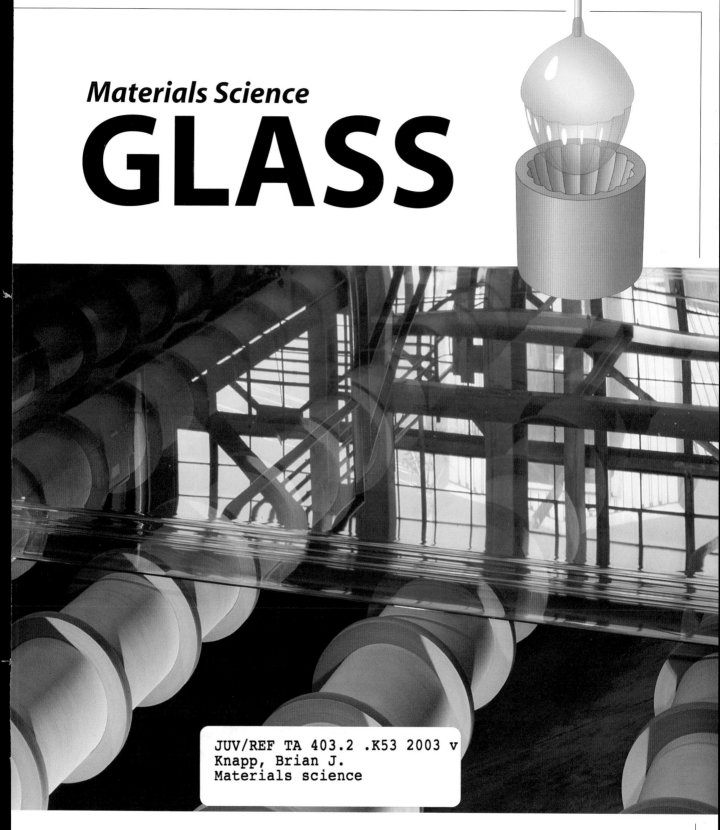

making use of the secrets of matter

Grolier
First published in the United States in 2003 by
Grolier, a division of Scholastic Library Publishing,
Sherman Turnpike, Danbury, CT 06816

Author
Brian Knapp, BSc, PhD

Industrial Consultant
Jack Brettle, BSc, PhD
(Head of Science Support Group, Pilkington Technology)

Art Director
Duncan McCrae, BSc

Senior Designer
Adele Humphries, BA, PGCE

Editors
Mary Sanders, BSc, and Gillian Gatehouse

Illustrations
David Woodroffe

Design and production
EARTHSCAPE EDITIONS

Scanning and retouching
Global Graphics sro, Czech Republic

Print
LEGO SpA, Italy

Library of Congress
Cataloging-in-Publication Data
Knapp, Brian J.

Materials science / Brian Knapp.
p. cm.
Includes indexes.
Summary: Presents the main scientific properties of materials
and how they are determined, as well as how substances can be
manipulated or modified to produce a wide array of materials
with an equally wide array of applications.
Contents: v. 1. Plastics—v. 2. Metals—v. 3. Wood and paper
—v. 4. Ceramics—v. 5. Glass—v. 6. Dyes, paints, and adhesives
—v. 7. Fibers—v. 8. Water—v. 9. Air.
ISBN 0-7172-5697-9 (set : alk. paper)
1. Materials—Juvenile literature. [1. Materials.
2. Materials science.] I. Title.

TA403.2.K53 2003
620.1'1—dc21

2002044537

Acknowledgments
The publishers would like to thank the following for their kind
help and advice: *Jack Brettle*; *The Corning Museum of Glass*;
Gordon Jones; *Kjc Operating Company*; *Pilkington plc*.

Picture credits
All photographs are from the Earthscape Editions photolibrary
except the following: (c=center t=top b=bottom l=left r=right)

Collection of The Corning Museum of Glass COVER background,
2-3 and 50-51t (float tank interior), 1, 51cr (float glass emerging
from annealer), 30 (vase), 33tl (ewer signed by Ennion), 33br
(glass blowing demonstration), 34 (Roman jar with handles),
36 (beaker with dolphins), 37bl (chamberstick), 37tr (goblet),
39tr source unknown (crown glass being spun); *Courtesy
Corning Incorporated, Corporate Archives* 43 (hot glass gob),
45 (light bulbs emerging from machine); *Collection of the
Rakow Research Library of The Corning Museum of Glass*
40 (background image of The Crystal Palace Exhibition,
1851); *NASA* 52; *Courtesy Pilkington plc* 40 inset (cylinder
factory interior), 27tl (press-bending assembly line); *UKAEA
Technology* 49br.

Contents

(*Left*) This is an extraordinary use of a glass bulb. The base has been removed without the glass imploding; it has been inverted and then used as a holder for oil as part of an oil lamp. This "inverted technology," in which a high-tech object is transformed for a different, low-tech use, is typical of recycling in developing countries. Great skill is employed to take an object that would require an expensive machine to produce and make something out of it by hand.

    The glass bulb, being transparent and nonreactive with oil, makes an excellent holder because the user can see when the reservoir needs to be refilled. (The base is made from the top of a metal aerosol can!)

1: Introduction

It is hard to imagine that GLASS has much to do with the sand on a beach. Yet the rough fragments of sand, which are completely OPAQUE, can be transformed into a material that is completely TRANSPARENT.

Nature made glass on Earth some four billion years ago. People began to make glass for themselves some 4,000 years ago. Since then people have discovered how truly versatile this material is, made more so by advances in understanding the science of how glass works and how it can be combined with other substances.

The unique nature of glass

Glass is a unique kind of material. Ask anyone what glass is, and they will almost certainly tell you without hesitation that it is a hard substance that you can see through. Ask them what it is used for, and they might give answers ranging from a lens in their glasses, a windowpane, an optical fiber, to a protective covering on the Space Shuttle.

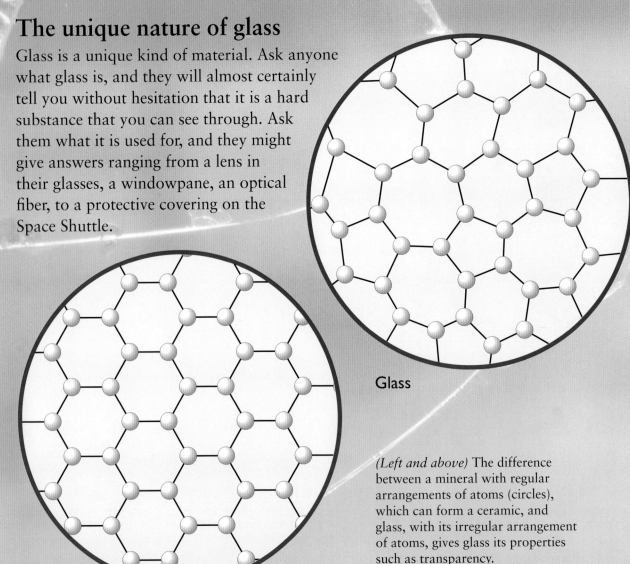

Glass

Crystal

(*Left and above*) The difference between a mineral with regular arrangements of atoms (circles), which can form a ceramic, and glass, with its irregular arrangement of atoms, gives glass its properties such as transparency.

See **Vol. 4: Ceramics** to find out more about the nature of ceramics.

Although it is so well known, glass is actually a very difficult material to put into any group with other materials. It is made from the same kind of materials that make cement, but it is not a crystalline mineral, or CERAMIC. It has some of the properties of a LIQUID (its ATOMS are not arranged in regular patterns) but also some of the properties of a SOLID (it is hard and cannot flow).

The uniqueness of the substance we call glass has led many people to put it into a category all of its own—a special state of matter—a GLASSY STATE. Others simply call it a special kind of solid—an AMORPHOUS solid, meaning that as it cools from being molten, its atoms lock together in an unorganized way and so cannot form perfect crystals.

(Below) Glass is often thought of as being both transparent and brittle. Many modern glasses are not as brittle as their historical counterparts because they have fewer defects in them.

Glass is so unusual because, unlike a metal in which the molten material turns immediately into a solid made of crystals on cooling, in a glass there is a steady and gradual change that stiffens the glass and traps the atoms before they can rearrange themselves into crystals. That is why, on a microscopic scale, the atoms have the same pattern as they had when they were liquid.

The same happens as the glass is heated—the glass softens steadily until it is finally all liquid, while metals suddenly change into a liquid.

This unorganized structure accounts for the fact that most glass is transparent. However, it is not only hard and dense, but also brittle. It is easily broken by a sudden blow.

All glasses break with a fracture, which often produces sharp knife or spearlike edges on the broken fragments.

(Above and below) Recycling of glass is only possible because glass can be remelted and re-formed time after time. The only thing that restricts its reuse is the amount of impurity in the glass being recycled. That is the reason you are asked to keep different colored glasses apart.

Glass contains no PORES and so does not let through either gases or liquids.

Glass tends to hold heat rather than conduct it. Cold glass is usually a poor conductor of heat and electricity (although a sheet of thin window glass is nowhere near as good an insulator as the wood or bricks of the walls in which it is set).

Glass will not easily react with other substances and so it can be used as a container for most acids and alkalis. It can also safely be used for holding medicines and foods.

See **Vol. 3: Wood and paper** to find out more about wood and insulation.

Natural glass

The most common kind of natural glass is obsidian. Obsidian is usually opaque because of the impurities found in it, but thin splinters can be transparent.

The properties of obsidian attracted Stone Age people, and obsidian sources became Stone Age "factories": The splinters of glass were used as scrapers, knives, and arrowheads. These shapes are made by striking one piece of obsidian against another, a process called knapping.

Obsidian became an important material that ancient peoples traded.

Natural glass can also be created in small quantities by lightning strikes and meteorite impacts—it is called tektites.

(Below) Stone Age people made scrapers, knives, and spearheads from obsidian.

(Left) Glass forms in nature. It is not especially transparent and normally looks black with a glassy sheen. It is called obsidian and is produced as part of volcanic eruptions.

The ingredients of glass

In industry glass is mostly made by combining sand (silicon dioxide—SiO_2), soda (sodium carbonate—Na_2CO_3), and lime (calcium oxide—CaO). However, there are many special glasses that contain a wide variety of other materials.

The most bulky ingredient (usually sand) is called a FORMER. The material that makes the former melt at a lower temperature (the soda in this case) is called a FLUX. The material (for example, lime) that stops the glass from crumbling, forming crystals, or dissolving is called a STABILIZER. They are all described in more detail below.

It is quite possible to make glass just by heating silica on its own to produce SILICA GLASS. But to do so, the temperature has to be raised to over 1,700°C. The energy needed for this is so high that pure silica glass is expensive. Nevertheless, cheaper glasses cannot match it for standing up to rapid temperature changes or for its low reactivity. It is also used to make some

Oxide ingredient in	Soda-lime glass
Silica (SiO_2)	73.6
Soda (Na_2CO_3)	16.0
Lime (CaO)	5.2
Potash (K_2O)	0.6
Magnesia (MgO)	3.6
Alumina (Al_2O_3)	1.0
Iron oxide (FeO)	–
Boric oxide (B_2O_3)	–
Lead oxide (PbO)	–

(*Above*) The composition of glass is given by its chemistry. All of the material used to make glass are oxides. In this table they are shown by percentage weight.

(*Below*) Laboratories need silica glasses to perform experiments that involve intense heating.

Oven glass	Lens glass	Silica glass
80.0	35.0	96.5
4.6	–	–
–	–	–
0.4	7.0	–
–	–	–
2.0	–	0.5
–	–	–
13.0	–	3.0
–	58.0	–

(Right) Much cut glass contains lead because it adds to the natural sparkle.

lenses for telescopes and glasses. Pure silica glass is made from quartzite and other pure forms of silica rather than sand.

Making glass at a lower temperature than is needed to make silica melt is one of the most important requirements in glassmaking. This is done by adding a material called a flux. Sodium oxide (Na_2O) is the flux used in much glassmaking. That is why soda is used in glassmaking. During heating, the soda changes from sodium carbonate to sodium oxide. The addition of a flux makes the silica molecules move slightly apart and so allows the silica to become more mobile. It also halves the temperature at which silica will melt. Potash (K_2O) and lithium oxide (Li_2O) are also used as fluxes.

Using a flux comes at a price. Glass made this way is quite soluble in water. To get over this problem, another ingredient—the stabilizer—is added: usually lime in the form of limestone, but litharge, alumina (Al_2O_3), magnesia ($MgCO_3$), barium carbonate ($BaCO_3$), strontium carbonate ($SrCO_3$), zinc oxide (ZnO), and zirconium oxide (ZiO) are all also used. Chemical reactions between the stabilizer, flux, and former make the glass almost insoluble.

Making glass is not just a matter of producing glass with suitable properties. The cost of glassmaking also has to be taken into account. So, scientists look for a compromise between good all-round properties and low cost in manufacture.

The proportions of 75% silica, 10% lime, and 15% soda produce a glass with good all-round properties. But variations from this standard formula are also important for specific common uses. For example, sheet glass (used for windows) has 6% lime and 4% magnesia (magnesium oxide, or MgO). Bottles, on the other hand, contain 2% alumina (aluminum oxide, or Al_2O_3).

Prince Rupert's Drop

In the 17th century this toy used to amaze the court of James the First of England and amuse his grandson Prince Rupert. It consisted of a curved droplet of glass made by dripping molten glass into cold water. As a result of rapid surface cooling, the surface tends to shrink fast while the inside is still hot. That leaves the glass under great stress.

The thick end of the drop can stand up to this stress and can even be struck with a hammer without breaking. However, the thin tail of the drop is much more fragile. If it is snapped off, that releases all of the stresses stored up in the drop, and the whole drop instantly shatters into a powder.

The prince would ask someone to hold the bulbous end of the drop, and then he would break off the thin tail. The glass would then explode in their hand, startling them. Because it disintegrated into a powder, this breakage was safe!

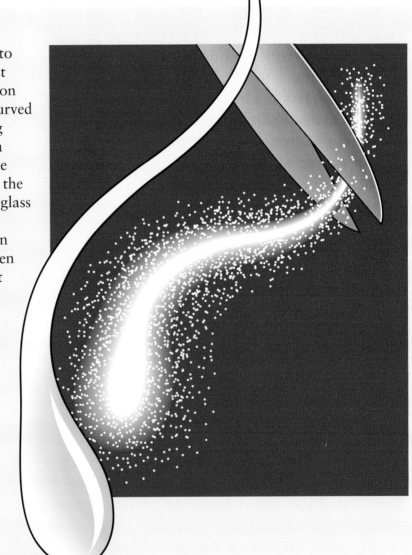

(Right) The need for glass shades on oil lamps helped stimulate the development of borosilicate glass.

Glasses manufactured by these methods tend to have a natural green tinge due to the presence of iron impurities in the sand used for the silica. If required, the tinting can be counteracted using a small amount of a decolorizer chemical. Selenium oxide (SeO_2), cobalt oxide (CoO), arsenic oxide (As_2O_5), and sodium nitrate (Na_2NO_3) are widely used for this. The result is a glass without any color sheen—so-called WHITE GLASS.

Soda lime glass and its variations are clear enough for windows and many other purposes, but the glass does not sparkle. However, a sparkle can be added by using lead monoxide (PbO) as a flux. Such a glass is heavier than soda glass; but when cut properly, it can be used to make extremely attractive table glass.

Giving glass special properties

Coloring glass

Because silica combines readily with metal oxides, they can be used to color glass. Typical oxides and colors are purple-blue from cobalt, green or yellow from chromium, yellow from uranium, and violet from manganese. Ferrous oxide (FeO_2) produces a green or a blue color, but it varies with the chemistry of the glass. Ferric oxide (Fe_2O_3) yields yellow glass. Lead oxide (PbO) and silver oxide (AgO) also add a yellow color. Nickel makes potash-lead glass violet but turns soda lime glass brown. Copper produces blue or green coloring depending on the amount of copper oxide.

(Right) Colored glasses are used for decoration in many modern buildings.

(Left) Most laboratory glassware is made from borosilicate glass.

(Below) Borosilicate glass—often more commonly known by the trade name Pyrex®—can be used for ovenware and even for glass saucepans (*above right*).

Making glass resist heat and cold

Glass behaves very differently than a metal. Most glass cannot expand and contract safely with changing temperature in the way that a metal can. Soda lime glass, for example, has quite a high coefficient of thermal expansion, meaning that is shrinks markedly when cooled and swells when heated. At the same time, it does not conduct heat well, and it has a low fracture stress value (it breaks easily). As the temperature falls, stresses build up inside that can make it break. So, for example, if cold water is poured onto a sheet of hot soda glass, the glass will almost certainly shatter.

(Right) Thermometers are made of borosilicate glass so that expansion of the glass does not lead to inaccurate measurements of temperature.

Glass made only from silica changes size very little when it is heated and cooled. It also has a high fracture stress value. It could be an ideal material to use if it were not so expensive and difficult to make.

The first attempts to make a heat-proof yet economical glass happened because it was hard to use lanterns in rainy conditions. If the lantern glass got hot from the candle or oil lamp inside and the lamp was taken outside, the rain falling on the hot glass shattered it.

As a result of experimentation, it was found that if borax (boric oxide B_2O_3) was added to the glass, it would not crack when cooled quickly. However, the borax made the glass very prone to corrosion with water. Just as soda glass is very weak without lime, so a stabilizer was needed for the new borax glass.

The stabilizer was found in 1912. It was alumina (aluminum oxide, Al_2O_3). The stabilizer also had the added, and unexpected, advantage of making the glass inert (unreactive) in the presence of food acids. This was discovered in 1914 when Jesse Littleton of the Corning Corporation was told of an emergency at home. His wife's ceramic baking dish had broken. Littleton sawed the top off a battery jar and gave it to his wife. In the end, Bessie Littleton cooked cakes in sawn-off battery jars and made custards in lamp chimneys. As a result, new heat-proof glass was manufactured for bakeware and sold under the trade name Pyrex®.

Going one step further, experiments showed that the new borosilicate glass was also inert in the presence of most industrial acids and alkalis. As a result, this new glass was also produced for laboratory glassware and is still used today. Glass fiber, ceramic glaze, and vitreous enamel are also borosilicates.

Borosilicate glass is made with 5 to 20% boric oxide (B_2O_3) replacing most of the sodium oxide (Na_2O), and with alumina (aluminum oxide (Al_2O_3)) replacing most of the lime (CaO).

(Below) The glass used to make light bulbs does not have to resist the rapid changes in temperature you might expect, even though the filament inside the bulb can reach a temperature of several thousand degrees in just a fraction of a second. As a result, it is made from soda lime-silica glass. That is a major factor in allowing light bulbs to be cheap. The glass bulb for a lamp is known in bulb making as a "shell."

Giving metal the properties of glass

Some of the properties of glass are extremely useful and can be added to the properties of another material. That happens with metal and glass.

Porcelain enameling, also called vitreous enameling, is a process of fusing a thin layer of glass to the surface of a metal object. It seals in the metal, prevents corrosion, and at the same time gives the metal an attractive glaze. Iron pots have been enameled for centuries. Enameled pots, pans, and bathtubs were developed in the 19th century and are still made **today**.

The problem with enamelware is that being made of glass, it can crack if the metal is dented. Metal has to be scrupulously clean if it is to be enameled. The enamel is applied (as in glazing pots) as a mixture of ground glass, clay, and water. The items are then fired in a furnace.

Glass ceramics

Glass is a material made by fully melting sand. A ceramic is a material made from clay that is heated in a furnace called a kiln to a lower temperature than is needed to make it fully molten. At this temperature some of the clay reacts, and it fuses together to produce a fired piece of pottery that is waterproof and hard.

But it is possible to make a material that has the properties of both glass and ceramic. It is called a GLASS CERAMIC.

A glass ceramic is made by heating glass to a much higher temperature than normal. It becomes an opaque solid that is extremely strong and much less liable to shatter. What happens is that microscopic crystals form, making the glass opaque but leaving it like a glass nonetheless. Most glass ceramics are made by encouraging the growth of microscopic crystals, which is achieved by adding a chemical called a NUCLEATING AGENT. A glass ceramic is therefore a crystallized glass with perhaps 98% crystals stuck together by the remaining glass phase at the crystal boundaries.

Glass ceramics are finding an increasing range of uses where high temperature resistance and great strength are needed—from special cookware to the warheads of missiles.

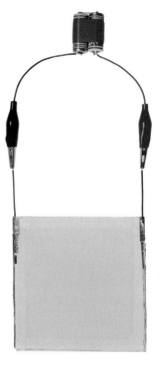

(Below) This special glass is darkened and lightened by applying a small electric current.

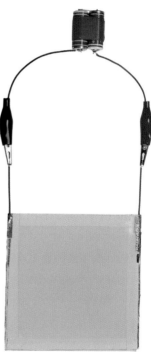

See **Vol. 4: Ceramics** *to find out more about glass ceramics.*

Making glass conduct electricity and become magnetic

Some glasses have very important electrical properties. They are known as chalcogenide glasses and contain such elements as thallium, arsenic, tellurium, and antimony. These glasses act as SEMICONDUCTORS and react to light.

By coating glass, it is possible to produce an even wider range of properties. For example, a thin coating of tin oxide helps the glass reflect heat but can be thin enough that the glass stays transparent. This can also improve the energy efficiency of the glass. In winter the coating reflects heat from inside back into the room, thereby reducing heat loss. Other coatings can be used to reflect the sun's heat in summer and keep a building cool. Such glass is found in the glass siding of many modern office blocks.

Glasses can also be made that have magnetic properties; they appear in computers and some transformers. They are metallic glasses—basically metals cooled so quickly they remain AMORPHOUS and do not develop crystal structure.

(Right) Most skyscrapers use glass with energy-efficient properties.

2: Properties of glass

Glass is a very versatile material, so there are many thousands of types of glass in regular production. It is versatile because so many of its properties can be varied. However, it is important to realize that when one property of glass is changed, that change will affect many other properties too.

Getting the right combination of properties can be an art as well as a science.

Chemical properties

Glass is made from three main chemicals: the FORMER, for example, sand; the flux, for example, soda; and the stabilizer, for example, lime. Together these three components (and any others that are added to give the glass special properties) make a material that is not only transparent (or colored if other chemicals are added) but also hard and almost corrosion proof.

One of the most important properties of glass is that it is almost inert (unreactive). Glass made many thousands of years ago has survived in underwater wrecks as well as buried in the soil. Although its surface may have suffered from some scuffing (abrasion) and some may have dissolved away, in general, the bulk of the glass remains intact.

Glass is still used because it has good resistance to corrosion. It can not only hold a wide variety of acids and alkalis, but also will not corrode when exposed to the air. Glass can be made into windows that will last and last or laboratory glassware that can be used over and over again.

(Left and above) Quite amazingly, although usually taken for granted, glass can stand up to strong acids and alkalis, and it is also resistant to flames that would destroy many other materials.

Glass is not entirely corrosion proof. Some extremely harsh acids and alkalis will attack it. They include hydrofluoric acid and concentrated phosphoric acid, hot concentrated alkalis, and superheated water.

The corrosive effect of hydrofluoric acid can be turned to advantage. It is actually used to ETCH the surface of glass, making decorative effects or a "ground glass" finish used in camera eyepieces and elsewhere.

Hydrofluoric acid is by far the most powerful of the corrosive acids; it attacks any type of silicate glass.

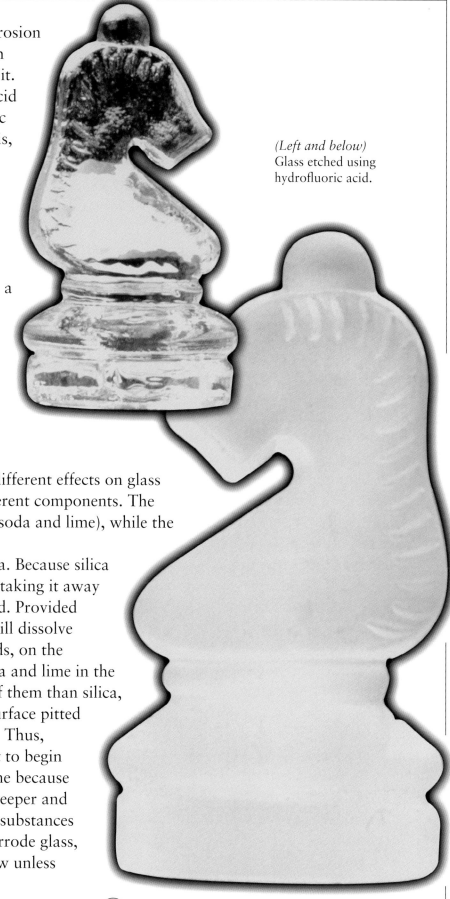

(Left and below) Glass etched using hydrofluoric acid.

Acids and alkalis have different effects on glass because they react with different components. The acids react with the alkalis (soda and lime), while the alkalis react with the silica.

Alkalis dissolve the silica. Because silica is such a large part of glass, taking it away leaves almost nothing behind. Provided there is sufficient alkali, it will dissolve glass at a constant rate. Acids, on the other hand, dissolve the soda and lime in the glass. Because there is less of them than silica, dissolving leaves the glass surface pitted and covered with tiny holes. Thus, while acid attack is very fast to begin with, it slows down over time because fresh acid has to penetrate deeper and deeper into the glass to find substances to attack. Water also can corrode glass, but the rate is extremely slow unless the water is superheated and only then is corrosion important. Observation windows used in boilers can be vulnerable to this kind of attack. Very often mica (which in thin sheets is also reasonably transparent) is used instead of glass or as an inner protective sheet to keep the water from the glass.

Finally, a few parts of alumina (aluminum oxide) in the glass composition greatly improves the way glass can stand up to attack by acids and alkalis.

Electrical properties

Glass is a NONMETAL. Like the majority of nonmetals, it is an insulator that has very high electrical resistance. Copper, for example, conducts electricity 10^{18} (ten million, million, million) times as well as glass.

In general, the electrical conductivity of glass increases with the proportion of soda, lime, and other alkalis in it.

On the other hand, some glasses are very good at storing electricity on their surfaces. This is an extremely important property because electrical charge storage devices called CAPACITORS are used in many electronic circuits.

Such glasses separate the metal plates of a capacitor by their good insulating properties.

Any glass that is developed for its electrical storage properties is known as a high-k glass.

Thermal properties

Glasses can be very good at holding heat compared with many substances, but still only a fifth to a third as good as water.

Glass is also a reasonable insulator of heat, but not as good as air. That is one reason why in double glazing air is used as the insulator trapped between two layers of glass.

Single-pane glass has no such insulating layer and therefore allows lots of heat to escape.

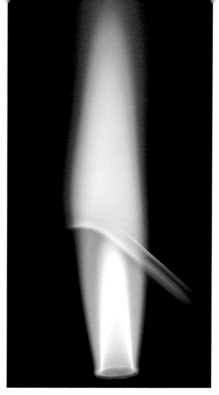

(Above) The sodium in glass can be identified by a flame test. The flame changes color as the glass melts, showing the typical orange color of the element sodium and the red color of the element calcium.

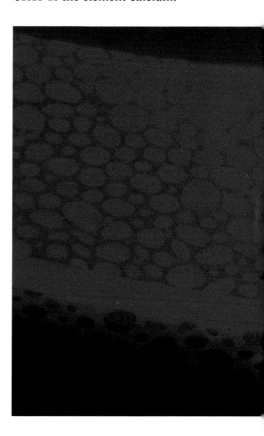

Expansion properties

Ordinary soda lime glass expands considerably when heated and shrinks when cooled. Because of this and because of the poor thermal conductivity of glass, if glass is suddenly heated or cooled (as, for example, plunging hot glass into cold water), the surface will try to expand or shrink much sooner than the middle. That will set up great stresses and lead to shattering.

Borosilicate glasses are normally used to get over this problem because they expand only a third as much as soda lime glass. However, it is possible to reduce swelling and shrinking almost to zero by adding 7.5% titanium oxide to pure silica glass. It appears in mirrors used in outer space, where temperature changes can be sudden and dramatic.

Heat is conducted through a solid material by conduction and radiation. Clear glass does not conduct heat better as it gets hot. Some types of glass, for example, glass ceramics, are transparent to infrared (heating) radiation and so can be used as stove burners.

(*Below*) Stove tops are made of glass ceramic and take advantage of its thermal and expansion properties. Glass ceramic is used because its thermal expansion coefficient is close to zero (it was originally developed for telescope mirrors in which distortion due to uneven temperature is a major issue). Because the expansion is close to zero, it resists thermal shocks such as spilling cold liquid on a hot plate. It is also hard (it has been used in body armor) and therefore resists scratching by abrasive cleaners. Finally, it is relatively transparent to infrared rays. Halogen bulbs or burner elements below the glass ceramic can heat the pan on top via infrared light transmitted through the burner and thus at the same time minimize heating of the burner itself.

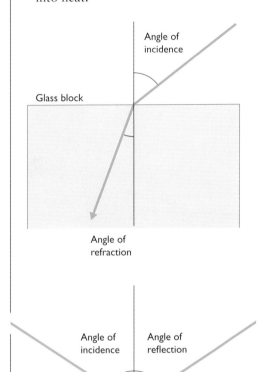

(Below) When light approaches glass, it may penetrate the glass or be reflected from its surface. If the light penetrates the glass, its angle of travel is changed. Not all light emerges from the glass. Some is absorbed and changed into heat.

Angle of incidence

Glass block

Angle of refraction

Angle of incidence

Angle of reflection

Mirror

Optical properties

When a beam of light falls on a piece of glass, some of the light is reflected from the glass surface, some of the light goes through the glass, and some is absorbed in the glass.

When light goes through glass, it is bent. That is called REFRACTION. The angle of refraction depends on the chemical composition of the glass. When the angle at which the light approaches (called the angle of incidence) is too steep, the so-called critical angle is reached, and after this the light is almost entirely reflected.

White light is a combination of the whole "rainbow" (spectrum) of visible colors. Each of the colors in this rainbow has a slightly different wavelength. When white light enters glass, each color in the light behaves differently. Each colored light is bent differently. Blue light bends more sharply than red light in the same glass, and the colors in between (green and yellow) are bent at angles between these extremes. The result is that the white light is split up into its spectrum of colors.

In a parallel-sided piece of glass these differences are not apparent because the bending that occurs when light enters the glass is balanced by the reverse bending as the light leaves the glass. However, when light enters a triangular glass block such as a prism, in which the sides are not parallel, the colors remain separated and show up as the spectrum.

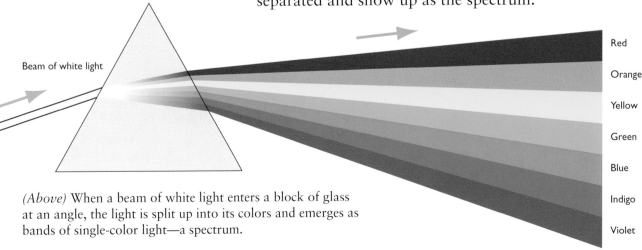

Beam of white light

Red
Orange
Yellow
Green
Blue
Indigo
Violet

(Above) When a beam of white light enters a block of glass at an angle, the light is split up into its colors and emerges as bands of single-color light—a spectrum.

Tinting glass

If glass is colored (by having metal oxides added to the melt), it will transmit some colors of white light and not others. Cobalt gives a blue tint to glass, chromium adds green, and manganese makes purple.

In traffic lights there is a white light behind each lens. The lenses are colored (using metal oxides) to absorb all colors except red in the red lens, amber in the amber lens, and green in the green lens. All other kinds of light are held back, absorbed, and changed to heat.

Glass will also selectively transmit waves of light beyond the range we can see. Lenses that transmit only ultraviolet or infrared light appear black to us. That is because they hold back all visible light.

Glass can also selectively hold back these invisible waves of light, allowing only visible light to get through. Heat filters in projection lamps work this way, keeping back the infrared rays so that the heat does not damage the film.

The amount of bending caused by a particular type of glass is called its REFRACTIVE INDEX. The higher the refractive index, the greater the bending. Lead glass has a much higher refractive index than soda lime glass.

Glasses are made with a wide range of refractive indexes. In a camera lens there may be seven different glasses stuck together to produce the effect the maker wants.

(Above) Some modern windshields are made of tinted glass, as shown here. Others have a shade band at the top. This localized color band is not actually in the glass but in the plastic interlayer in the safety LAMINATE used for windshields.

(Above) Traffic lights use colored glass to act as filters for all parts of the spectrum except the color they show.

(Above) Metallic reflective sunglasses use a metal film so thin you can see through it.

(Below) If you look at the surface of a lens, you can often catch a glimpse of the surface coatings used.

Surface coating glass

Optical effects can be changed even further by coating the surface. That is done, for example, in sunglasses as well as in camera lenses. The greatest reflectance occurs when there is a thick metal coating; then the glass simply becomes a supporting material for the metal—it is a mirror. Very thin metal coatings are put on metallic reflecting sunglasses. In this way a little light gets through even though they appear to be totally reflecting.

When light strikes a piece of glass at a glancing angle, it can be totally reflected. That makes the glass act as a mirror, which can be undesirable, especially, for example, in camera lenses. As a result, special coatings can be added that make the glass almost unreflective, allowing all light to get into the glass no matter at what angle it strikes.

Holograms

By adding small amounts of cerium oxide and copper, silver, or gold, glass can be made to behave in special ways. For example, when ultraviolet radiation is shone on it and the glass is reheated, changes in refractive index over microscopic distances can be made to occur that may be seen as strong colors. This technique can be used to produce HOLOGRAMS.

Photochromic glass

Most eye glasses use lead-silicate glass. To make glasses that react to light (called PHOTOCHROMIC GLASSES), less than a tenth of 1% silver halide and copper is added. When light shines on the glass, the silver halide changes to metallic silver. The silver then clumps together into tiny grains. These grains are still small enough to allow people to see through the glass, but dense enough for the glass to look brown or gray. When less light falls on the glass, the chemical changes reverse, and the glass lightens again.

Mechanical properties

Because the atoms in glass are not arranged in regular patterns as they would be in a crystal, they do not fit together as well. As a result, silica glass (with no additives) is slightly less dense than a crystal of the same material (for example, quartzite). However, both calcium from lime and sodium

Glass with a "silvered" back, such as in a car mirror (*below*) or the solar reflectors (*above*), is used for the reflecting properties of the metal. The glass is simply a support that also prevents the metal from TARNISHING.

from soda will fit in the space in the dissolved silica glass structure, and so soda lime glass is actually denser than natural crystal.

Glass is known for its brittleness. But it is not entirely brittle and will bend a little, as you will notice if you see people carrying a large pane of glass. This is known as ELASTICITY. In fact, most glass bends a little, for example, a windshield glass bends under the pressure of the wind as a car moves at speed. Glass will twist and stretch as well as bend, but again, only a little.

If most materials are pulled or twisted further, they will change shape and not go back to their starting point. This is called PLASTICITY. Finally, if the material is bent, twisted, or stretched enough, it will break. Glass is unusual in that it goes almost immediately from its elastic state to breaking. It has almost no plasticity.

Glass is very strong when compressed but much weaker when it is stretched by being bent, pulled, or twisted. There is not much difference between the strength of all glasses due to the different chemicals in them, but strength can be greatly affected by surface imperfections. Just as a scratch mark cut by a diamond tip creates a line of weakness along which the glass will break cleanly, so a scratch on the surface of a glass will be a place at which stress builds up.

Defect-free glass is much stronger than any metal. However, glass is rarely defect free. As mentioned above, it has surface flaws and minute scratch marks or contamination of the surface, for example, by handling with fingers. They can reduce the strength of glass by a thousand times when it is pulled, although they do not affect it when the glass is squashed.

The strength of glass also varies depending on how long it has to support a weight.

When glass breaks, or fractures, the crack starts at the weakest point and then travels outward. That is true even when a piece of glass appears to explode or shatter.

Strengthening glass

There are several ways to make glass stronger and less liable to break.

One way is to remove all the surface scratches (including the ones you cannot see) by polishing the glass. Glass can also be "glazed," that is, a thin layer of another glass is fused onto the surface. This thin layer is made of glass that swells and shrinks less than the main piece of glass.

When the glass that has been glazed is heated or cooled quickly, the surface swells or shrinks less and so puts the surface under compression—which is when glass is strongest.

Remember that glass cannot be broken by compression forces, only by pulling (tension) ones. In glass that is compressed on the surface, the middle of the glass compensates by going under tension. But since this region of tension is in the middle of the

(Below) There is almost nowhere more vulnerable than the glass used in car headlights. The glass catches the force of the wind and rain as well as dirt and stones from the road. If the glass were soft, it might scratch easily and so scatter the light. Headlight glass has to be hard and tough.

In this picture you are looking through the headlight glass to the glass of the bulb. The other materials protected by the headlight glass are the silvered plastic reflector and the orange plastic diffuser used to turn a light sideways for road safety.

glass, safe from blows and bumps, that makes the glass less liable to break. When glass is treated in this way, it can also take greater loads than when it is unstressed. It is called toughened glass.

Toughened glass can also be obtained by putting glass under stress while it is being made. In this case the whole surface is under compression. This is called tempering. Tempered glass is often a legal requirement in

places where glass could cause injury, for example, in double glazing of doors and shower glass. Tempered glass breaks into a large number of rounded pieces rather than into long, sharp shards.

To stress glass by tempering, it has to be heated until it is almost soft, then cooled very quickly in a controlled way. The inside cools after the outside so that the inside is still trying to cool and shrink when the outside of the glass has already set hard. That is what causes the pulling stress toward the center, at the same time compressing the surface.

Glass can also be made safer by laminating it, as for example, in car windshields. Bulletproof glass is often laminated, or layered. Laminated glass is a sandwich of glass and plastics. The inner part of the sandwich is made of a tough plastic. Not only does the plastic layer help absorb the energy of an impact, but the fact that the glass is stuck to the plastic reduces the chances of sharp shards flying away and injuring people.

Glass can also undergo CHEMICAL STRENGTHENING. In this method it is placed in a hot bath (500°C) containing potassium nitrate. Potassium atoms are larger than the sodium atoms in the glass. When the glass is hot, sodium atoms will swap places with potassium atoms close to the surface. Then, when the glass cools, the larger potassium atoms more than fill the spaces between the silicon atoms, leading to compression and strength. This process is used to strengthen eyeglass lenses and also aircraft windows.

(Above) Wire-reinforced glass.

(Below) Modern windshields are designed to resist breaking when they are hit by stones. Usually, they just chip and the chip can be filled in with a liquid plastic.

(Above) Fractures move outward from the point of impact. This windshield is on an old car. The glass was only strengthened, and any crack immediately crazed the whole windshield.

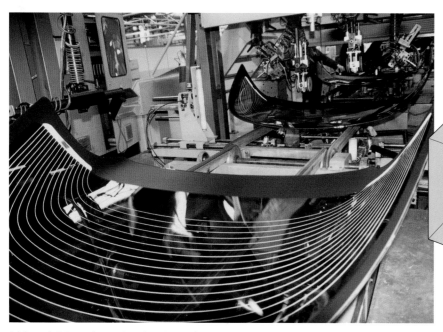

(*Above*) Manufacturing laminated glass windshields.

(*Right*) During the manufacture of a three-layered windshield, an opaque plastic sheet is put between two sheets of perfectly matching transparent glass. The three sheets are heated under pressure. The plastic turns transparent and sticks to the glass to form the reinforced windshield.

(*Below*) A crack in laminated glass. The crack comes from a stone hitting the windshield. Notice that the crack is only on the outer layer and that the whole windshield has not shattered. This is an important safety factor for drivers.

(*Right and below*) A laminated glass seen from the side, showing the sandwich of layers.

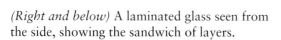

3: Glass through the ages

Glassmaking was one of the earliest industries. It was even the very first industry in America. In 1608 the newly arrived colonists in Jamestown, Virginia, began making glass for export back to England using the sand from the seashore.

Glass was first made in the ancient world somewhere in the Middle East perhaps about 2500 B.C. It was in the form of small beads. By 1450 B.C. glass bottles were being made in Egypt. They already had the combination of sand and soda common in most modern glass. Bottles were often decorated with a zigzag pattern.

From Egypt the art of glassmaking spread around the shores of the Mediterranean Sea, arriving in Greece by the 9th century B.C. As Alexander the Great forged a new empire that stretched to India, glassmaking spread into Asia. As a result, by 200 B.C. glass beads were being made in India.

Ancient glass

Almost as soon as people began to melt metal, they began to make glass. However, although sand melted and made glass in the hearths used to melt copper metal, it was unrecognizable as a special material and thrown away as part of the unwanted waste products.

At some point, however, someone noticed that glass was an attractive material. This probably did not happen during metalworking. It might have happened when people heated their pottery in order to make it hard and workable. Here, too, are the high temperatures needed to make sand melt. Or could it have been by accident around a wood fire set for cooking on a seashore? That might have produced just the right conditions for the sand to melt and form into beads at lower temperatures because the ash from wood fires acted as the source of the flux.

Glassmaking instructions

People treasured their skills at making glass. From time to time they wrote down instructions about how to make glass, which we can still read today.

Early glassmaking had little science to help it, and so it was a mixture of luck, skill, and trusting in the gods. In fact, more attention is given to pleasing the gods than to preparing the glass mixture.

Glassmaking instructions begin by telling people to choose a favorable month and then look for a good omen.

Only then should the furnace be built and blessed by putting religious objects near it. To make sure the glass is even more likely to be good, sacrifices of sheep should be made, incense burned, and an offering of honey and butter put out for the gods. After this has been done, the fire can be lighted.

Special wood should be chosen for the fire, for example, poplar wood without its bark.

The glass mixture should be of finely ground quartz and plant ashes. Once it has been made up, the fire can be started. Once the mixture turns yellow, it is ready to be poured out.

Whatever the first discovery, from this time on, for thousands of years the raw materials for making glass were the same—a mixture of sand, wood (the source of soda), and crushed seashells—the source of lime.

Crucible glass

Soon people learned that glass could more conveniently be made in a crucible—a dish made out of clay that could be put on a fire. But an open-topped crucible will not allow temperatures to get high enough for glass to form properly. Furthermore, the natural materials in clay contaminated the glass with other chemicals. As a result, pure glass, and especially clear glass, could not be made. This was a problem only solved in later centuries by using extremely pure materials.

Because glass is difficult to make, people began to specialize: Some operated furnaces and made the glass in bulk; others took the raw glass and reheated it and fashioned it into finished goods.

You can get an idea of the scale of this glassmaking from the slab of glass preserved at the Beth She'arim cemetery in Galilee, Israel, in the 4th century A.D. The glass slab found here was abandoned after it had been made and is still intact thousands of years later. It is nearly 3 m long and weighs 9 tons.

To produce this slab would have needed probably 20 tons of wood fuel and 11 tons of sand and lime. The whole mixture would have been fired in a pit and might have taken 10 days to melt and form.

The slab would have provided the glass for tens of thousands of drinking glasses or bowls.

Cast glass

The first glass was all cast. That is, it was melted and then poured into a mold, or ground glass was heated in a mold until it melted. This produced only solid objects. It could not, for example, result in a bottle. To make a bottle, the glass had to be formed around a solid object called a core (see opposite).

Whether solid or hollow, the surface would have been very rough because it would have taken on the surface texture of the clay mold.

Glass cast in this way therefore had to be smoothed, for example, by rubbing it with pieces of sandstone rocks. Some glass was smoothed and polished by turning it on a LATHE. It was all hard, time-consuming work.

The labor and time that went into glass meant it was a precious material and only available to the wealthy.

Molded glass

By 100 B.C. people had discovered how to press molten glass into a mold and so get it to take on the shape of the mold.

(*Below*) The Egyptians had mastered the art of core forming by the middle of the 16th century B.C. (see opposite). This vase belongs to the 18th Dynasty, around 1400 to 1300 B.C. It is about 11 cm tall.

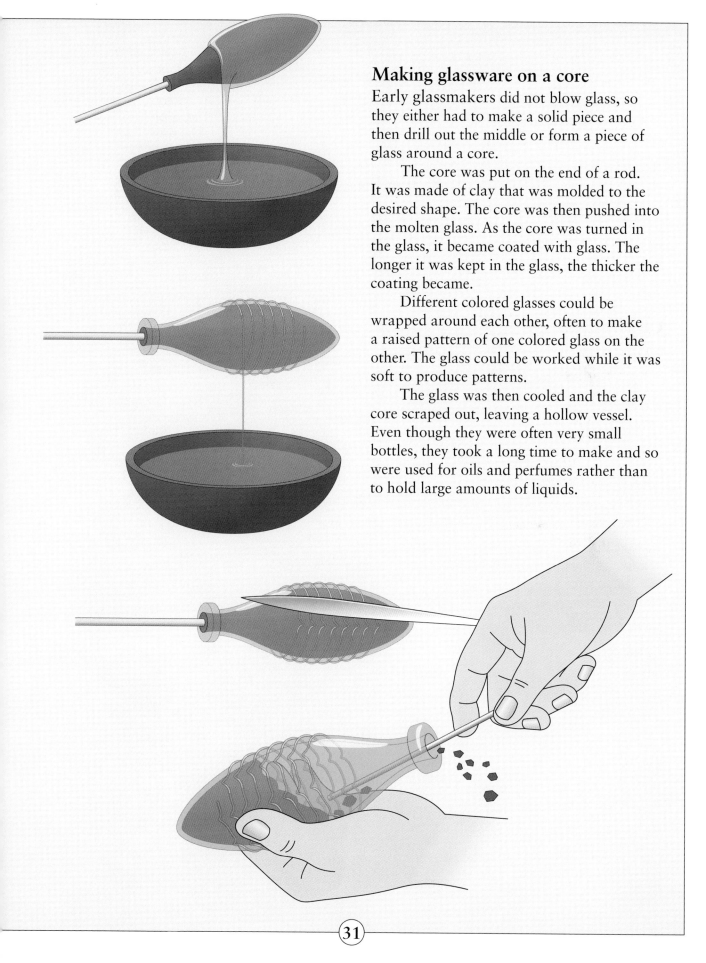

Making glassware on a core

Early glassmakers did not blow glass, so they either had to make a solid piece and then drill out the middle or form a piece of glass around a core.

The core was put on the end of a rod. It was made of clay that was molded to the desired shape. The core was then pushed into the molten glass. As the core was turned in the glass, it became coated with glass. The longer it was kept in the glass, the thicker the coating became.

Different colored glasses could be wrapped around each other, often to make a raised pattern of one colored glass on the other. The glass could be worked while it was soft to produce patterns.

The glass was then cooled and the clay core scraped out, leaving a hollow vessel. Even though they were often very small bottles, they took a long time to make and so were used for oils and perfumes rather than to hold large amounts of liquids.

The first blown glass

Blowing glass avoids the problem of surface roughening because there is usually no mold to blow into. The Phoenicians (who lived in modern Syria in about the first century B.C.) were the first to learn how to blow glass through an iron tube with a blob, called a GOB, of molten glass on the end. The tube (blowing iron) was about 1.5 m long.

They also learned how to make enclosed, or pot, furnaces that could be heated to a far higher temperature than open furnaces. That meant glass could become fully molten.

One end of the tube was rolled in glass inside the furnace to get a gob of glass to stick to it. The gob was then rolled out on an anvil (perhaps into a long sausage shape for a bottle), and then it was blown freely in air. Glass could also be put into a smooth-sided (for example, steel) mold and then blown so that it pressed out on the sides of the mold. Such techniques are still in use today.

In addition to the blowing iron, a bar of iron was used to help in the shaping. It could push at the glass or carry

new pieces of glass—for example, handles—to the work so they could be fused in place.

Colored glass

By 100 B.C. developments in glassmaking were taking place at Alexandria, Egypt, in North Africa. By using natural earths (which are colored by metal oxides), glass rods could be made in various colors. Copper oxide produced a green and red glass; iron oxide made black, brown, and green glass; antimony oxide yielded a yellow color; while manganese produced purple-colored glass.

Pieces of these rods then were formed into patterns just as small pieces of stone are used to make a mosaic floor. The most famous look like flowers and are called millefiori, meaning "thousand flowers." In this process the shape of the bowl was made of mud and the glass stuck into it. The glass and core were then put in an oven so that the glass partly melted and fused together. The glass was cooled and the mud scraped away. The rough surface of the glass was then ground smooth.

Despite all of these successes, people found it impossible to make flat glass. The only alternative was to use small pieces of glass and to hold them together

(Below) Many modern craftspeople use techniques almost identical to the way glass was blown and molded thousands of years ago.

(Left and above) By 50 B.C. the technique of glass blowing had been invented. The bubble of glass could be shaped by rolling it along the ground or blowing it into a mold. This would produce more intricate shapes than with cast glass. Glassblowing enormously speeded up the manufacture of glass. This jar is about 24 cm tall and was made in about the first century A.D.

with another material, for example, lead. Thus a difficulty in coping with the science of glassmaking resulted in some of the most beautiful of all works of colored glass art—glass mosaics in Roman times and the stained glass windows in churches and other buildings by the 12th century. (The reason that it is called stained glass is that stains were fused to the surface of the glass; the whole glass was not colored.)

In later centuries people continued to experiment with getting reliable and rich colors. Johann Kunckel in Germany found that ruby-red glass could be made using gold chloride. To get the chloride, gold was dissolved in aqua regia (a mixture of concentrated sulfuric and hydrochloric acids).

(Right) The beauty of stained glass depends on the colors produced by the glassmaker. Medieval stained glass of the 12th to 14th centuries was made by cutting out tiny pieces of colored glass and then attaching them to one another with lead. It was a time-consuming and delicate art. The colors were obtained by using molten metal oxides such as cobalt to produce blue and antimony for yellow. Even the sheets of glass did not begin as sheets at all but were made as bubbles of colored glass that were elongated into cylinders and then cut down their length and flattened out while the glass was still hot and therefore plastic. In this way small sheets about 30 cm across were produced.

Although this technique of stained glassmaking has been much copied since, it has never been equaled because of the extraordinary amount of labor involved in both making the glass and then assembling the pieces. "Modern" stained glass uses special "antique" glass made in traditional ways, although quite often the colors as well as the images are painted onto clear glass rather than made up as a mosaic.

(Left) The Romans made a wide range of colored glasses. This jar is about 12 cm tall. It was made by applying random fragments of colored glass to a premade jar. The jar was probably rolled in the colored glass fragments and then reheated until the glass softened so that the fragments flattened out. The jar could then be blown bigger so that the flattened fragments of glass were stretched into this attractive pattern.

the wife of Richard Smailes
born xvi Nov: mdccclxiii

of this parish of Goathland
and died x July mcmxxvii

Getting furnaces hotter

By the 10th century pot furnaces had also developed further and consisted of three compartments: one to hold the molten glass and two others next to it to allow the glass to be cooled slowly once objects had been made. Finished articles were put in the hotter of the two finishing compartments for a while and then transferred to the cooler one before being taken out and left in cool air.

Interestingly, many of the pot furnaces were built without any way of getting a draft of air through them. That is why these furnaces never reached very high temperatures. Later on, glass furnaces would become very tall cones, some over 30 m high. The change in design was specifically to get a blast of air through the furnace and to increase its temperature.

Decolorizing glass

Although it was desirable to give glass attractive colors, it was also desirable to remove the natural greenish hue from plain glass that is caused by iron impurities. The Romans discovered that by adding antimony or manganese to the glass, they could get close to colorless glass. These oxides produce a complementary color to the green of iron oxide, and that results in a neutral gray tinge to the glass. Otherwise, an opaque white glass (looking something like ground glass) was made using tin oxide.

In the 15th century Venetian glassmakers perfected the use of a manganese compound called pyrolucite in their glass. It became known as "glassmaker's soap" because it "cleaned" the glass of accidental colors. However, glass with pyrolucite is not clear and colorless. It has a grayish tinge and is poorly transparent.

The Venetian glassmakers got over these problems by making articles in very thin glass in which the color and lack of transparency would not be noticed. Again, the scientific limitations were overcome in a way that resulted in glass of exquisite quality in craftsmanship.

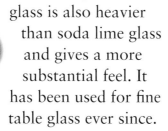

Crystal glass

Gradually the Venetians learned how to make a form of crystal glass that has a sparkling clear quality. It was called *cristallo*. Like crystal glass made later elsewhere, it was produced by using purer ingredients that had far less color and so did not have to be decolorized. A potash-lime glass was particularly clear. It became known as Bohemian crystal after the region of central Europe where it was developed.

The next development took place in London in 1674, when lead oxide was added to the mix. George Ravenscroft produced lead crystal glass this way, sparklingly clear glass still in use today. Lead glass is so sparkling because it has a very high refractive index. The advantage of lead crystal glass was that it was softer than soda lime glass and so could more easily be cut (to make cut glass, which sparkles in light) and also engraved. Lead glass is also heavier than soda lime glass and gives a more substantial feel. It has been used for fine table glass ever since.

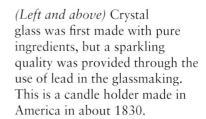

(Left and above) Crystal glass was first made with pure ingredients, but a sparkling quality was provided through the use of lead in the glassmaking. This is a candle holder made in America in about 1830.

(Above) Glassmaking for scientific and decorative purposes developed greatly in the 19th century but relied on hand skills.

Science revolutionizes glassmaking

Virtually all of these advances over the millennia had been made by trial and error, with virtually no understanding of the science of glass. But by the 18th century that began to change.

In 1830 Jean-Baptiste-André Dumas in France was able to analyze glass chemically and show that the best ratio for ingredients in soda lime glass were one part soda, one part lime, and six parts silica sand.

Improving ingredients

As much as anything, understanding the chemistry of glass allows its raw materials to be made reliably in a factory rather than having to deal with natural materials. For example, the development of a chemical process called the SOLVAY PROCESS produced huge quantities of soda ash (sodium carbonate) of consistent quality. Similarly, the formulas for colors were discovered, allowing them to be produced reliably as well. Lime could also be produced from kilns using limestone rather than from crushed seashells. Potash, too, could be made artificially.

One of the results of this scientific revolution was that the cost of glass fell dramatically, and so it could be bought and used by more and more people.

The next stage in the scientific revolution had to wait a century until it was possible to understand the atomic structure of glass. Following the work of W. H. Zachariasen, it was possible for the first time to understand that glass is a solid with disordered atoms.

Crown glass

Making clear, flat glass proved to be one of the most difficult things to achieve either by hand or by machine. From Roman times until the 17th century flat glass was made by pouring it over a flat surface and rolling it flat while it was still in a plastic state. But this still did not produce glass that was of even thickness. After the dangerous act of rolling, the glass was allowed to cool but still had to be ground by hand.

There was another way to make flat glass, known as crown glass. To make it, the glassmaker blew the glass into a bubble that had cylindrical sides. A rod was then attached to the bubble, and the rod and bubble spun quickly. That caused the bubble to change shape into a flat piece of glass. As part of this process, the center of the bubble collapsed down to a cone-shape. We now call these pieces bull's-eyes. To save wastage, they could be used for the occasional window pane even though it was impossible to see clearly through the bull's-eye. Today, bull's-eyes are made specially for their decorative effect.

The crown method did not produce very large pieces of glass, which is one reason small windows appeared with many glazing bars holding them in place. Again, a difficulty was turned into an advantage through the beautifully proportioned Georgian window frames that made best use of the glass sizes available.

(Above) Spinning a bubble of glass to make crown glass. The bull's-eye is seen as the place where the disk attached to the rod.

(Below) This colored bulls-eye has been used decoratively in a stained-glass window.

Cylinder glass

An alternative that produced larger glass pieces, for example, for mirrors, was not to spin the bubble but to allow a giant cylinder to cool slightly, then cut it lengthwise. As it was reheated, the cylinder of glass spread out into a sheet.

(Below) The Great Exhibition of 1851 in London was held in the Crystal Palace. It required 300,000 panes of glass. All were made by the cylinder process. The construction used a third of England's entire glass production for a year. However, following this exhibition, people's views of how glass could be used changed forever.

(Below) Early forms of making flat glass began by producing huge cylinders of glass that were laid flat, cut open, and reheated so they changed into sheets. Despite all of this effort, the quality of the glass was not high, and irregularities in the thickness led to many distortions.

Learning to save fuel and money

In the middle of the 19th century the Siemens and Chance brothers in England began to think about ways to reduce the amount of fuel that was consumed in furnaces. By recycling the heat from furnaces, they were able to reduce the fuel used to a tenth of that needed by earlier methods. As a result, glassmaking became cheaper again, and so its uses grew.

(Left, above, and below) The revolutions in glass are shown in these pictures. When glass was expensive and could only be made in small pieces, windows were tiny. As glass became more affordable, windows grew larger, and stores in particular could have fine frontages. But the fact that glass still could not be made in large pieces meant that the windows had to be divided up by glazing bars.

Finally, with the invention of plate glass made by the flotation process, huge sheets of glass could be made that were not only big but also strong enough to stand up to blows. Thus the changing face of our buildings owes as much to changes in glass technology as to any other part of the building revolution.

4: Machine-made glass

Glass is an extremely versatile material, and its uses are almost endless. However, in each application the glass has to stand up to a particular set of physical and chemical demands. Here you will see some modern examples of this.

The development of standard machine-made glass

Making glass by hand can result in exquisite objects, but it is both time consuming and extremely skilled work. Making glass by hand also has severe limitations. Glass objects cannot be produced cheaply, they cannot be of uniform size (that is, you cannot have standardization), and certain items, for example, large sheets of flat window glass, cannot be made at all.

Imagine trying to use glassware for chemical experiments when every glass object was of a different size. Each one would have to be measured separately. Furthermore, the chemist could not rely on having glassware that behaved the same way each time. This gives you some idea of the need to find methods for standardizing the making of glass.

Even if handmade glass could be standardized, the cost of labor would still make its use very limited. That is why mechanized ways of making glass were sought. The pioneering work for this was done in America at the start of the 20th century.

If you are going to mechanize glassmaking, you have to reproduce

The modern glass furnace

A modern glass furnace uses everything that has been learned from the past and the best available science.

The material going into the furnace (the charge) is a mixture of basic new ingredients and between 25 and 60% cullet, or crushed rejected glass of the same composition as the glass being made. The cullet not only recycles material, but it melts sooner in the furnace, which helps bring the fresh mineral particles together and so speeds up the glassmaking process.

Temperatures in a glass-melting chamber of a furnace depend on the glass being made, but would typically be 1,475°C for a soda lime-silicate glass.

While the glass is forming, large amounts of gas are given off from the reaction of the raw materials. These gases, together with the air already in the furnace, can cause problems because they can form bubbles in the glass.

Although large bubbles generally float to the surface, small bubbles are harder to remove. They have to be taken out in the next part of the furnace, called the conditioning chamber.

In the conditioning chamber the glass is slightly cooled (to perhaps 1,300°C for soda-lime silicate glass). The small bubbles disappear as they dissolve back into the glass. Mechanical mixers stir the melt to ensure it is all of the same quality.

the stages that a glassblower might go through. That is, you need to get the ingredients necessary for glass, you need to mix them, then heat them in a furnace, and then you need to shape them and finally slowly cool the finished articles.

Mass production works best if the raw material arrives in a steady stream. In this case the raw material is molten glass, and it is pushed out through a nozzle of the furnace (it is extruded) like toothpaste from a tube.

1. Containers

Containers such as bottles and light bulbs have to be made singly. As a result, the glass flow has to be changed so that small, precisely measured pieces, or gobs, of glass are fed into the shaping machines.

The shaping machines are essentially complicated molds. The glass is blown to shape once it is inside the mold.

Different objects require different-sized gobs of glass. This amount of glass is decided by setting the time interval for giant shears to cut the glass into pieces.

The cutting is arranged to coincide with the arrival of a mold. The gob of glass falls into the mold and is either pressed or blown into shape depending on which article is needed. Fantastic speeds can be achieved by some modern machines.

(Above) Gob of glass falling into the mold before being blown into shape.

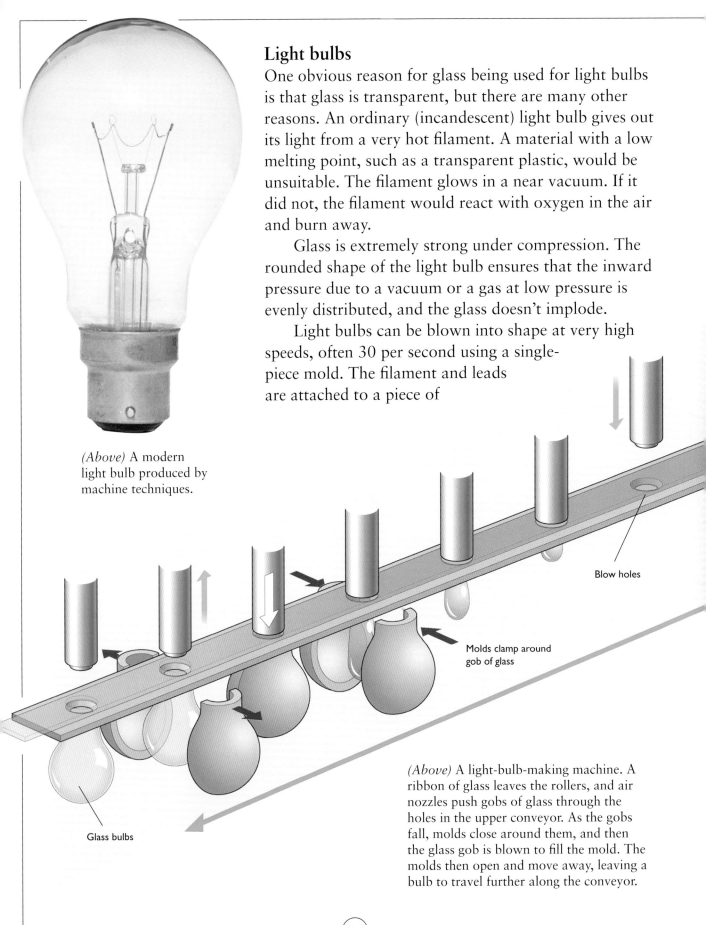

Light bulbs

One obvious reason for glass being used for light bulbs is that glass is transparent, but there are many other reasons. An ordinary (incandescent) light bulb gives out its light from a very hot filament. A material with a low melting point, such as a transparent plastic, would be unsuitable. The filament glows in a near vacuum. If it did not, the filament would react with oxygen in the air and burn away.

Glass is extremely strong under compression. The rounded shape of the light bulb ensures that the inward pressure due to a vacuum or a gas at low pressure is evenly distributed, and the glass doesn't implode.

Light bulbs can be blown into shape at very high speeds, often 30 per second using a single-piece mold. The filament and leads are attached to a piece of

(Above) A modern light bulb produced by machine techniques.

Blow holes

Molds clamp around gob of glass

Glass bulbs

(Above) A light-bulb-making machine. A ribbon of glass leaves the rollers, and air nozzles push gobs of glass through the holes in the upper conveyor. As the gobs fall, molds close around them, and then the glass gob is blown to fill the mold. The molds then open and move away, leaving a bulb to travel further along the conveyor.

Glass ribbon

Water-cooled
rollers

glass called a flare that holds the filament in the center of the bulb.

Glass can be sealed easily. The bulb is made with a neck that is attached to a vacuum pump. As the air is drawn out of the bulb, a flame melts the glass of the neck to the flare and so seals the bulb. This is a fast, easy, and cheap way of creating an airtight seal.

Light bulbs can be made of ordinary glass because although the glass heats up quickly, that compresses the glass, making it strong. When the light is turned off, the glass cools slowly, and so the chance of failure (thermal shock) is small.

Bottles

Bottles have been used as containers since about the third century A.D. However, for them to come into widespread use, production had to be made faster, and there had to be significant demand for them. The demand was brought about with the invention of the carbonation process for making "soda pop" in the 1770s. The fizzy drink needed to be put into convenient containers that would stand up to the stress of the pressurized water and also be clean and preferably reusable. This was the event that stimulated the bottling industry.

The scale of the change to mass production was staggering. At the Great Exhibition of London in 1851 alone a million bottles of pop were sold. Beer followed in Denmark in 1870 when a special pasteurization process had been developed that prevented the beer from spoiling. Bottled milk was also pasteurized, although the process was not widely used for this purpose until the 20th century.

Bottles with narrow necks cannot be made in a single stage. Instead, they are made in two stages. In the first stage the bottle is partly blown into shape by compressed air. The bottle is then transferred to a second mold where it is blown to the final shape. Each stage takes about 10 seconds.

Once molded, the bottles are sprayed with tin chloride solution. It produces a thin film of tin oxide, which hardens the surface and helps the glass resist blows and rubbing when transported. Then a thin plastic is spayed on to make the glass work more easily in bottling machines.

One problem in using bottles was how to hold a cap on firmly. Many bottles had caps that were wired on (as sparkling wine corks still are today). But two developments changed this for most bottles. In 1858 John Mason developed a machine for molding a screw thread onto a bottle, and narrow neck bottles were developed by 1885. After this it was possible to screw a metal cap directly onto the bottle.

(Right) How automated bottling plants work. The gob of glass drops into a mold and is forced to the bottom with compressed air. Compressed air is then blown up from the bottom of the mold, partly forming the shape. The partly formed bottle is then transferred to a different mold where the blowing process is completed. The final mold spins so there is no seam on the outside of the bottle.

(Left) Bottles are the next most important glass product after window glass.

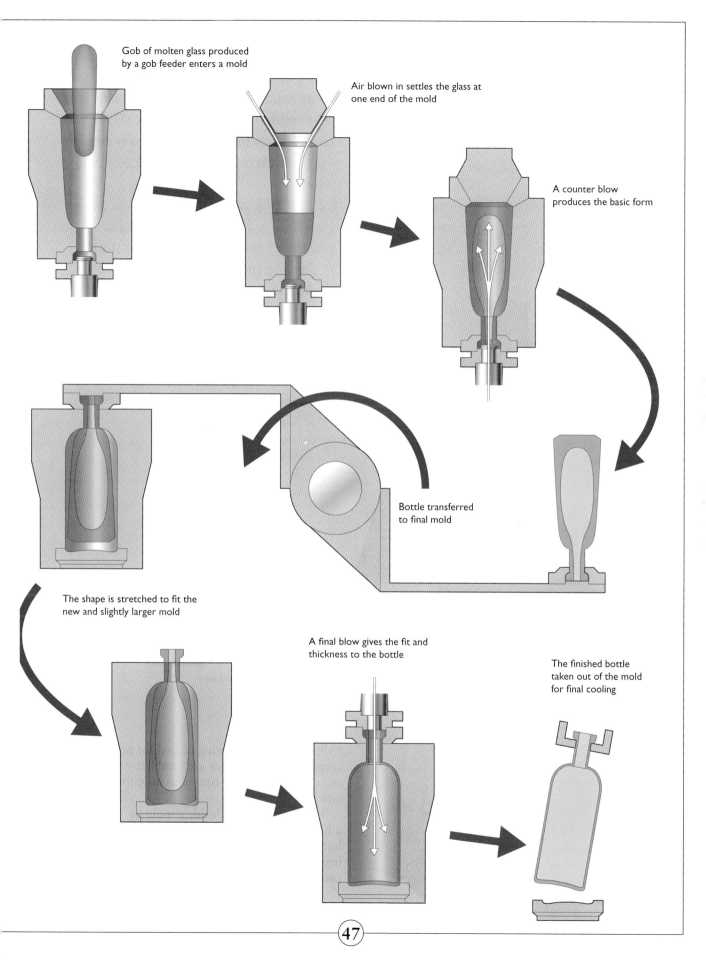

Gob of molten glass produced by a gob feeder enters a mold

Air blown in settles the glass at one end of the mold

A counter blow produces the basic form

Bottle transferred to final mold

The shape is stretched to fit the new and slightly larger mold

A final blow gives the fit and thickness to the bottle

The finished bottle taken out of the mold for final cooling

Tumblers

The most common forms of glassware on the table are tumblers for water or other beverages. Tumblers need to stand up to blows while being washed, yet they need to sparkle when clean. Soda lime-silicate glass is fine for this purpose, but tumblers need a shiny finish better than that used on bottles.

Tumblers are made by blowing gas into a mold. The mold is made of two halves and is lined with wetted sawdust or cork. As the glass is blown into the mold, it causes the water in the mold liner to turn to steam. This keeps the glass from touching the mold and so gives a smooth finish to the glass. The mold is then opened and the glass taken out and put on a conveyor belt. At this stage it has a sharp rim. It is rounded over, or beaded, using a flame that plays on the glass as it moves along the conveyor.

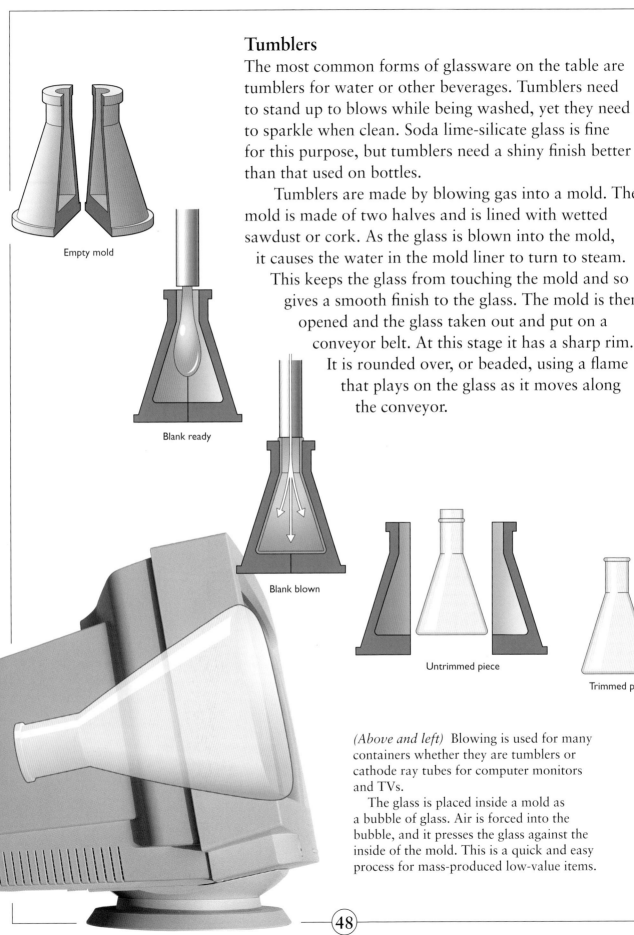

Empty mold

Blank ready

Blank blown

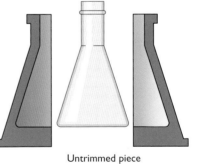

Untrimmed piece

Trimmed piece

(Above and left) Blowing is used for many containers whether they are tumblers or cathode ray tubes for computer monitors and TVs.

The glass is placed inside a mold as a bubble of glass. Air is forced into the bubble, and it presses the glass against the inside of the mold. This is a quick and easy process for mass-produced low-value items.

2. Flat glass

Plate glass

The earliest flat glass was made by casting glass (see page 30). It was poured out into a shallow tray. Roman buildings had windows made in this way. However, the surface was very rough, and it was poorly transparent.

Blowing glass into a disk (crown glass, see page 39) cannot produce glass of even thickness. Eventually, however, machines were developed that produced a ribbon of glass of even thickness. This kind of glass became known as PLATE GLASS, and it was developed at the start of the 20th century. It was first cast and then drawn through rollers.

The scale of this process could be huge, with a ton of glass being cast at a time.

The rollers determined the thickness of the glass. The process of rolling glass took away some of the clarity of the glass, so after rolling, it had to be ground and polished while it was moved along a conveyor. The grinding and polishing were an unwelcome stage in the process, using up huge amounts of energy and making about as much waste glass as finished product.

Float glass

To get over the problem, the float glass method was developed by Alastair Pilkington in 1959. In this case the glass is allowed to flow out onto the surface of a bath of molten tin. Surface problems do not occur in this process, and so no grinding and polishing are needed.

Tin was chosen because of its properties. It hardly reacts with the glass (and even when it does, tin oxide on the surface adds to its strength), it has a low melting point (232°C) but a high boiling point, and therefore it remains liquid over a broad temperature range.

Other metal alloys can be used instead of tin to widen the range of types of glass that are produced this way.

(Above) Plate glass used in store windows.

(Below) Float glass in windows.

(Above) Specialized high lead content glass in windows for laboratories handling nuclear materials.

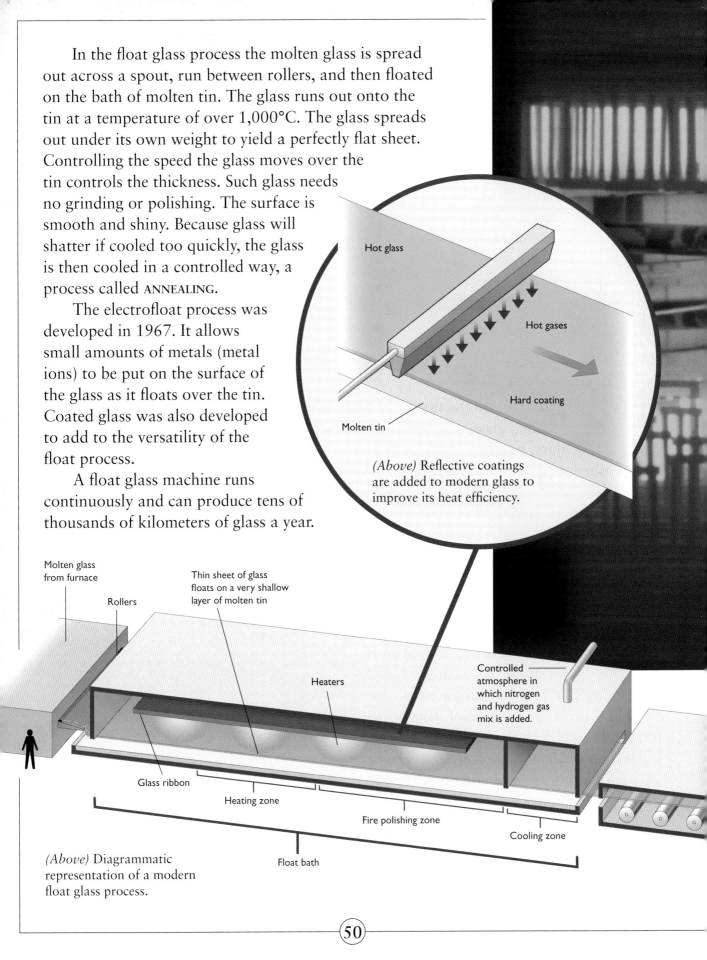

In the float glass process the molten glass is spread out across a spout, run between rollers, and then floated on the bath of molten tin. The glass runs out onto the tin at a temperature of over 1,000°C. The glass spreads out under its own weight to yield a perfectly flat sheet. Controlling the speed the glass moves over the tin controls the thickness. Such glass needs no grinding or polishing. The surface is smooth and shiny. Because glass will shatter if cooled too quickly, the glass is then cooled in a controlled way, a process called ANNEALING.

The electrofloat process was developed in 1967. It allows small amounts of metals (metal ions) to be put on the surface of the glass as it floats over the tin. Coated glass was also developed to add to the versatility of the float process.

A float glass machine runs continuously and can produce tens of thousands of kilometers of glass a year.

Hot glass

Hot gases

Hard coating

Molten tin

(Above) Reflective coatings are added to modern glass to improve its heat efficiency.

Molten glass from furnace

Rollers

Thin sheet of glass floats on a very shallow layer of molten tin

Heaters

Controlled atmosphere in which nitrogen and hydrogen gas mix is added.

Glass ribbon

Heating zone

Fire polishing zone

Cooling zone

Float bath

(Above) Diagrammatic representation of a modern float glass process.

(Below) Inside a modern float glass machine.

(Right) Float glass being annealed.

Diamond- or tungsten-carbide-tipped cutters

Robots stack glass vertically

Lehr (a furnace for annealing glass)

The Space Shuttle and International Space Station

Glass has many important roles in space. The most obvious is in the windows. The Space Shuttle has 37 triple-glazed window panes. The Space Station has hundreds.

The outer panes on the front of the cockpit of the Space Shuttle are silica glass. That is because they have to stand up to the very high temperatures experienced during reentry through the atmosphere.

The inner panes are made from an alumina-rich glass: a high-strength glass that acts as the strong pane that can withstand the difference in pressure between the cabin and the vacuum in space.

The middle panes are a thick silica glass. They are safety panels, able to stand up both to high reentry temperature and pressure. They are there in case the outer panels break.

However, the Space Shuttle has more glass than just its windows. The tiles that cover the bottom, sides of the tail, and parts of the wingtops of the Space Shuttle, and which take the high reentry temperatures, are coated in glass powder called SINTER or FRIT.

The most common use of glass in space is in very thin glass cover slips on solar cells. The glass contains cerium, which absorbs x-rays and prevents radiation damage to the solar cells beneath and also acts as a barrier to micrometeroid damage.

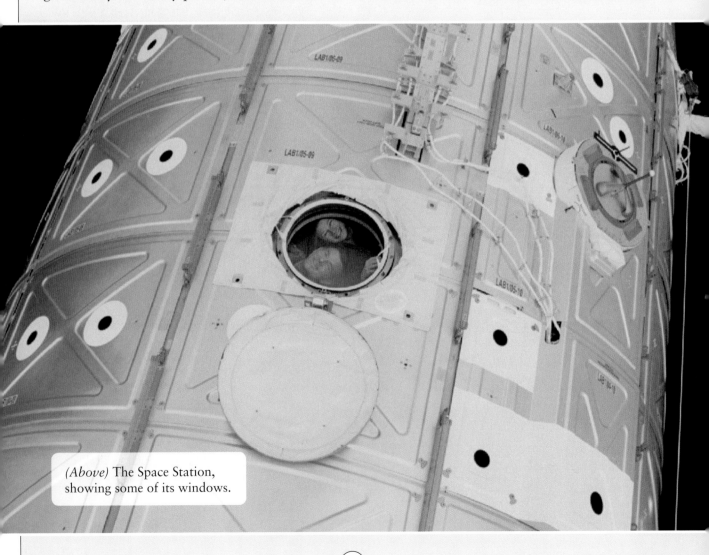

(Above) The Space Station, showing some of its windows.

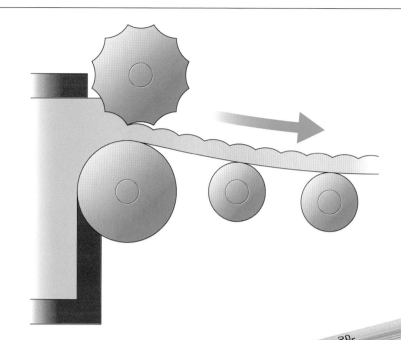

(Above and right) Rolling is used when glass with a texture is needed, for example, in flat glass used in bathroom windows. Rollers are made with special ridges. As the glass moves between them, the pattern is pressed into the glass.

(Above) Glass tubes are used for making thermometers.

3. Tubes and rods

Tubes and rods can be made in several ways. Essentially, glass is pushed through a hole or allowed to fall from a hole over a special cone-shaped piece of metal called a mandrel. Compressed air flows through the mandrel, and that opens up the glass into a tube.

Glass tube and rod can be made extremely quickly by this method. Production rates can exceed 60 km/hr of tube from each machine.

(Left) Tubes and rods are drawn over a cylinder or cone called a mandrel. Air is blown through the mandrel, and that holds the tube open until the glass has solidified. Rods are also drawn, but no air pressure is used.

4. Shaped glass

Many glass objects are complicated shapes that could not be produced by blowing. Headlights come from a gob of molten glass pressed in a mold. Windshields are flat pieces of glass that are heated to soften them a little and then pressed into a mold (press bending) or sagged into a mold under their own weight (sag bending). Both are a means of bending a piece of glass without damaging its surface; the glass is not made to flow as a molten gob would be.

(Below) Headlights are made by pressing the glass into shape in a mold. This is especially useful when thick glass pieces are needed. Pressing produces a better surface finish than blowing.

(Above) Shaped windshield glass.

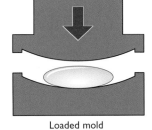
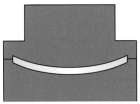

| Empty mold | Loaded mold | Glass pressed | Finished piece |

(Right) Fiberglass is used as home insulation.

See **Vol. 1: Plastics** and **Vol. 7: Fibers** to find out more about glass fiber.

(Below) Glass fibers can be embedded in a plastic (resin) to produce a strong, lightweight material. Fiberglass is easy to mold into shapes such as this canoe.

5. Fiberglass

Fiberglass is a glass fiber wool. It is used for building insulation. Glass fibers are produced in the same way as plastic fibers, by forcing the molten glass through a die with holes in it called a spinneret. The glass comes out in long strands and is whirled around by the spinning die. A blast of cold air cools the fibers, and they break into short lengths. An adhesive is sprayed onto the fibers so they can be formed into long mats.

Glass fiber can also be made into cloth using a spinneret. But in this case the fibers are not broken into pieces but pulled out and wound onto a drum. They can then be woven.

Glass fiber is long-lasting as well as fireproof.

6. Lens glass

Glass lens eyeglasses are mainly lead-silicate glass. They are also sometimes called flint glass.

When making lens glass, it is vital to have exact control of the way that light moves through the glass. That controls the magnification and clarity of the lens and its usefulness to the wearer.

High lead content glass is used because it bends the light strongly (it has a high refractive index). To achieve this, exceptionally pure materials have to be used.

Lens glass is normally melted in an electric furnace using platinum metal to line the furnace. This reduces the chances of impurities getting into the melt. The glass is poured out into molds that resemble lenses and so need relatively little finishing.

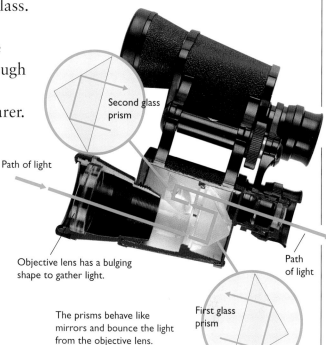

(Below) Reflected light rays through lenses and prisms of a pair of binoculars.

Second glass prism

Path of light

Objective lens has a bulging shape to gather light.

The prisms behave like mirrors and bounce the light from the objective lens.

First glass prism

Path of light

(Below) How eyeglasses work for both near- and far-sightedness.

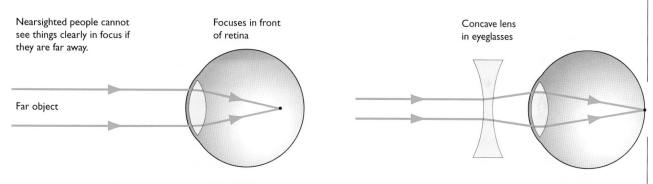

Nearsighted people cannot see things clearly in focus if they are far away.

Focuses in front of retina

Far object

Concave lens in eyeglasses

A concave lens is used for people who cannot see things in focus when they are at a distance. In this case the lens of the eye brings light to a focus in front of the back of the eye. The glass lens slightly diverges the light, so that the eye lens can then bring objects to a focus on the back of the eye.

A convex lens is used for people who cannot see things in focus when they are very close. This is the more usual eye problem. In this case the lens of the eye brings light to a focus behind the back of the eye. The glass lens slightly converges the light, so that the eye lens can then bring objects to a focus on the back of the eye.

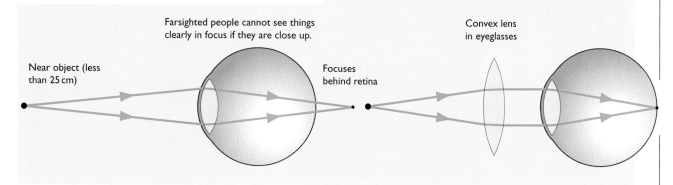

Farsighted people cannot see things clearly in focus if they are close up.

Convex lens in eyeglasses

Near object (less than 25 cm)

Focuses behind retina

More and more lens glasses are, however, being made of plastic because of weight. The light bending you can achieve per unit weight is important to the wearer.

7. Telescope lenses and mirrors

Telescopes lenses require the highest grade of optical glass. Instead of making a large telescope lens out of a single piece of glass as was done in the past, modern telescope optics are made from small balls of high-purity glass that are fused together to make the disk the lens is ground from.

Even mirrors (which use a silver coating on glass) need high-precision glass. The largest telescope glass in the world (at Mauna Kea, Hawaii) is 8.31 meters in diameter, 22 cm thick, and weighs 33 tons. It was made from very low expansion glass in fused pieces and then ground to the right shape before having a surface coating added.

8. Optical fibers

Glass many times thinner than a human hair is used to carry signals at the speed of light. This is the fastest, most reliable, and most modern way of transmitting information in the digital age. Most long-distance phone, TV, and computer data lines use optical fibers.

For long fibers to work, information is sent in the form of pulses of light through a fiber core. The core is sheathed in glass that has a lower refractive index than the core—the glass is made so that its properties change from the center to the outside. This arrangement ensures that as the light tries to leak out of the core, the light rays are bounced back into the core. In effect, the outer sheath of glass acts like a mirror. A single beam of light needs a fiber just ten millionths of a meter (microns) in diameter. Multiple beams can be sent in cores of diameter 50 microns or larger. Multiple beams (called multimode) are used for short-distance communication, with simple beams (monomode) used for long-distance communications, with many signals pulsed down the same simple beam at the same time.

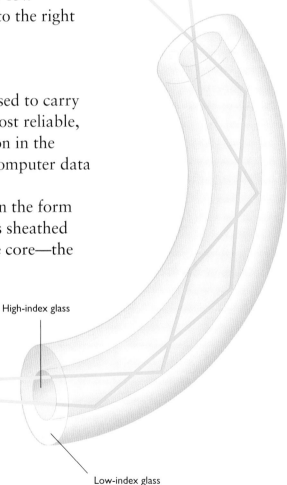

Beams of light

High-index glass

Low-index glass

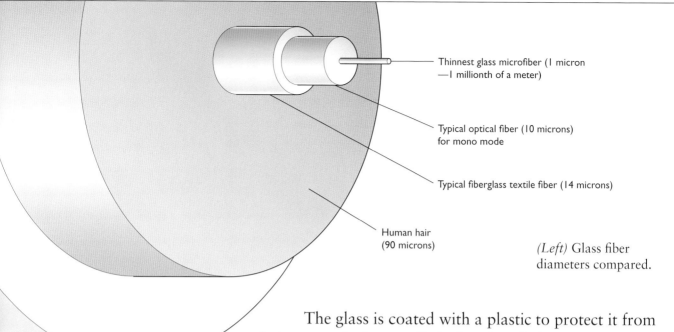

Thinnest glass microfiber (1 micron
—1 millionth of a meter)

Typical optical fiber (10 microns)
for mono mode

Typical fiberglass textile fiber (14 microns)

Human hair
(90 microns)

(Left) Glass fiber
diameters compared.

Glass optical communications
fiber to carry multiple beams
(50–125 microns or larger)
for multimode use

The glass is coated with a plastic to protect it from being scratched or scuffed when handled.

Optical fibers have many advantages over traditional copper wires. They are lighter, they can carry more information, they take up less space, and the signals travel faster. The glass melts at a higher temperature and so is resistant to melting in fires. Signals also fade more slowly in glass than in copper, and so there can be longer distances before the signals need to be amplified.

For fibers to be effective, the glass must be very pure; it must be free of bubbles or any surface defects.

Optical signals are sent by LASER. Optical fibers can transmit tens of thousands of telephone calls or computer communications at the same time.

(Left and right)
Optical fibers transmit
light along their
lengths. Optical fibers
are being installed
across the country to
allow improvements
in modern
communications.

Set Glossary

ACID RAIN: Rain that falls after having been contaminated by acid gases produced by power plants, vehicle exhausts, and other man-made sources.

ACIDITY: The tendency of a liquid to behave like an acid, reacting with metals and alkalis.

ADDITION POLYMERIZATION: The building blocks of many plastics (or polymers) are simple molecules called monomers. Monomers can be converted into polymers by making the monomers link to one another to form long chains in head-to-tail fashion. This is called addition polymerization or chain polymerization. It is most often used to link vinyl monomers to produce, for example, PVC, or polyvinyl chloride polymer.
See also **CONDENSATION POLYMERIZATION**

ADHESIVE: Any substance that can hold materials together simply by using some kind of surface attachment. In some cases this is a chemical reaction; in other cases it is a physical attraction between molecules of the adhesive and molecules of the substance it sticks to.

ADOBE: Simple unbaked brick made with mud, straw, and dung. It is dried in the open air. In this form it is very vulnerable to the effects of rainfall and so is most often found in desert areas or alternatively is protected by some waterproof covering, for example, thatch, straw, or reeds.

ALKALI: A base, or substance that can neutralize acids. In glassmaking an alkali is usually potassium carbonate and used as a flux to lower the melting point of the silica.

ALKYD: Any kind of synthetic resin used for protective coatings such as paint.

ALLOY: A metal mixture made up of two or more elements. Most of the elements used to make an alloy are metals. For example, brass is an alloy of copper and zinc, but carbon is an exception and used to make steel from iron.

AMALGAM: An alloy of mercury and one or more other metals. Dentist's filling amalgam traditionally contains mercury, silver, and tin.

AMPHIBIOUS: Adapted to function on both water and land.

AMORPHOUS: Shapeless and having no crystalline form. Glass is an amorphous solid.

ANION: An ion with a negative charge.

ANNEALING: A way of making a metal, alloy, or glass less brittle and more easy to work (more ductile) by heating it to a certain temperature (depending on the metal), holding it at that temperature for a certain time, and then cooling to room temperature.

ANODIZING: A method of plating metal by electrically depositing an oxide film onto the surface of a metal. The main purpose is to reduce corrosion.

ANTICYCLONE: A region of the Earth's atmosphere where the pressure is greater than average.

AQUEOUS SOLUTION: A substance dissolved in water.

ARTIFACT: An object of a previous time that was created by humans.

ARTIFICIAL DYE: A dye made from a chemical reaction that does not occur in nature. Dyes made from petroleum products are artificial dyes.

ARTIFICIAL FIBER: A fiber made from a material that has been manufactured, and that does not occur naturally. Rayon is an example of an artificial fiber.
Compare to **SYNTHETIC**

ATMOSPHERE: The envelope of gases that surrounds the Earth.

ATOM: The smallest particle of an element; a nucleus and its surrounding electrons.

AZO: A chemical compound that contains two nitrogen atoms joined by a double bond and each linked to a carbon atom. Azon compounds make up more than half of all dyes.

BARK: The exterior protective sheath of the stem and root of a woody plant such as a tree or a shrub. Everything beyond the cambium layer.

BAROMETER: An instrument for measuring atmospheric pressure.

BASE METAL: Having a low value and poorer properties than some other metals. Used, for example, when describing coins that contain metals other than gold or silver.

BAST FIBERS: A strong woody fiber that comes from the phloem of plants and is used for rope and similar products. Flax is an example of a bast fiber.

BATCH: A mixture of raw materials or products that are processes in a tank or kiln. This process produces small amounts of material or products and can be contrasted to continuous processes. Batch processing is used to make metals, alloys, glass, plastics, bricks, and other ceramics, dyes, and adhesives.

BAUXITE: A hydrated impure oxide of aluminum. It is the main ore used to obtain aluminum metal. The reddish-brown color of bauxite is caused by impurities of iron oxides.

BINDER: A substance used to make sure the pigment in a paint sticks to the surface it is applied to.

BIOCERAMICS: Ceramic materials that are used for medical and dental purposes, mainly as implants and replacements.

BLAST FURNACE: A tall furnace charged with a mixture of iron ore, coke, and limestone and used for the refining (smelting) of iron ore. The name comes from the strong blast of air used during smelting.

BLOWING: Forming a glass object by blowing into a gob of molten glass to form a bubble on the end of a blowpipe.

BOLL: The part of the cotton seed that contains the cotton fiber.

BOILING POINT: The temperature at which a liquid changes to a vapor. Boiling points change with atmospheric pressure.

BOND: A transfer or a sharing of electrons by two or more atoms. There are a number of kinds of chemical bonds, some very strong, such as covalent bonding and ionic bonding, and others quite weak, as in hydrogen bonding. Chemical bonds form because the linked molecules are more stable than the unlinked atoms from which they are formed.

BOYLE'S LAW: At constant temperature and for a given mass of gas the volume of the gas is inversely proportional to the pressure that builds up.

BRITTLE: Something that has almost no plasticity and so shatters rather than bends when a force is applied.

BULL'S EYE: A piece of glass with concentric rings marking the place where the blowpipe was attached to the glass. It is the central part of a pane of crown glass.

BUOYANCY: The tendency of an object to float if it is less dense than the liquid it is placed in.

BURN: A combustion reaction in which a flame is produced. A flame occurs where gases combust and release heat and light. At least two gases are therefore required if there is to be a flame.

CALORIFIC: Relating to the production of heat.

CAMBIUM: A thin growing layer that separates the xylem and phloem in most plants, and that produces new cell layers.

CAPACITOR: An electronic device designed for the temporary storage of electricity.

CAPILLARY ACTION, CAPILLARITY: The process by which surface tension forces can draw a liquid up a fine-bore tube.

CARBOHYDRATES: One of the main constituents of green plants, containing compounds of carbon, hydrogen, and oxygen. The main kinds of carbohydrate are sugars, starches, and celluloses.

CARBON COMPOUNDS: Any compound that includes the element carbon. Carbon compounds are also called organic compounds because they form an essential part of all living organisms.

CARBON CYCLE: The continuous movement of carbon between living things, the soil, the atmosphere, oceans, and rocks, especially those containing coal and petroleum.

CAST: To pour a liquid metal, glass, or other material into a mold and allow it to cool so that it solidifies and takes on the shape of the mold.

CATALYST: A substance that speeds up a chemical reaction but itself remains unchanged. For example, platinum is used in a catalytic converter of gases in the exhausts leaving motor vehicles.

CATALYTIC EFFECT: The way a substance helps speed up a reaction even though that substance does not form part of the reaction.

CATHODIC PROTECTION: The technique of protecting a metal object by connecting it to a more easily oxidizable material. The metal object being protected is made into the cathode of a cell. For example, iron can be protected by coupling it with magnesium.

CATION: An ion with a positive charge, often a metal.

CELL: A vessel containing two electrodes and a liquid substance that conducts electricity (an electrolyte).

CELLULOSE: A form of carbohydrate. *See* CARBOHYDRATE

CEMENT: A mixture of alumina, silica, lime, iron oxide, and magnesium oxide that is burned together in a kiln and then made into a powder. It is used as the main ingredient of mortar and as the adhesive in concrete.

CERAMIC: A crystalline nonmetal. In a more everyday sense it is a material based on clay that has been heated so that it has chemically hardened.

CHARRING: To burn partly so that some of a material turns to carbon and turns black.

CHINA: A shortened version of the original "Chinese porcelain," it also refers to various porcelain objects such as plates and vases meant for domestic use.

CHINA CLAY: The mineral kaolinite, which is a very white clay used as the basis of porcelain manufacture.

CLAY MINERALS: The minerals, such as kaolinite, illite, and montmorillonite, that occur naturally in soils and some rocks, and that are all minute platelike crystals.

COKE: A form of coal that has been roasted in the absence of air to remove much of the liquid and gas content.

COLORANTS: Any substance that adds a color to a material. The pigments in paints and the chemicals that make dyes are colorants.

COLORFAST: A dye that will not "run" in water or change color when it is exposed to sunlight.

COMPOSITE MATERIALS: Materials such as plywood that are normally regarded as a single material, but that themselves are made up of a number of different materials bonded together.

COMPOUND: A chemical consisting of two or more elements chemically bonded together, for example, calcium carbonate.

COMPRESSED AIR: Air that has been squashed to reduce its volume.

COMPRESSION: To be squashed.

COMPRESSION MOLDING: The shaping of an object, such as a headlight lens, which is achieved by squashing it into a mold.

CONCRETE: A mixture of cement and a coarse material such as sand and small stones.

CONDENSATION: The process of changing a gas to a liquid.

CONDENSATION POLYMERIZATION: The production of a polymer formed by a chain of reactions in which a water molecule is eliminated as every link of the polymer is formed. Polyester is an example.

CONDUCTION: (i) The exchange of heat (heat conduction) by contact with another object, or (ii) allowing the flow of electrons (electrical conduction).

CONDUCTIVITY: The property of allowing the flow of heat or electricity.

CONDUCTOR: (i) Heat—a material that allows heat to flow in and out of it easily. (ii) Electricity—a material that allows electrons to flow through it easily.

CONTACT ADHESIVE: An adhesive that, when placed on the surface to be joined, sticks as soon as the surfaces are placed firmly together.

CONVECTION: The circulating movement of molecules in a liquid or gas as a result of heating it from below.

CORRODE/CORROSION: A reaction usually between a metal and an acid or alkali in which the metal decomposes. The word is used in the sense of the metal being eaten away and dangerously thinned.

CORROSIVE: Causing corrosion, that is, the oxidation of a metal. For example, sodium hydroxide is corrosive.

COVALENT BONDING: The most common type of strong chemical bond, which occurs when two atoms share electrons. For example, oxygen O_2.

CRANKSHAFT: A rodlike piece of a machine designed to change linear into rotational motion or vice versa.

CRIMP: To cause to become wavy.

CRUCIBLE: A ceramic-lined container for holding molten metal, glass, and so on.

CRUDE OIL: A chemical mixture of petroleum liquids. Crude oil forms the raw material for an oil refinery.

CRYSTAL: A substance that has grown freely so that it can develop external faces.

CRYSTALLINE: A solid in which the atoms, ions, or molecules are organized into an orderly pattern without distinct crystal faces.

CURING: The process of allowing a chemical change to occur simply by waiting a while. Curing is often a process of reaction with water or with air.

CYLINDER GLASS: An old method of making window glass by blowing a large bubble of glass, then swinging it until it forms a cylinder. The ends of the cylinder are then cut off with shears and the sides of the cylinder allowed to open out until they form a flat sheet.

DECIDUOUS: A plant that sheds its leaves seasonally.

DECOMPOSE: To rot. Decomposing plant matter releases nutrients back to the soil and in this way provides nourishment for a new generation of living things.

DENSITY: The mass per unit volume (for example, g/c^3).

DESICCATE: To dry up thoroughly.

DETERGENT: A cleaning agent that is able to turn oils and dirts into an emulsion and then hold them in suspension so they can be washed away.

DIE: A tool for giving metal a required shape either by striking the object with the die or by forcing the object over or through the die.

DIFFUSION: The slow mixing of one substance with another until the two substances are evenly mixed. Mixing occurs because of differences in concentration within the mixture. Diffusion works rapidly with gases, very slowly with liquids.

DILUTE: To add more of a solvent to a solution.

DISSOCIATE: To break up. When a compound dissociates, its molecules break up into separate ions.

DISSOLVED: To break down a substance in a solution without causing a reaction.

DISTILLATION: The process of separating mixtures by condensing the vapors through cooling. The simplest form of distillation uses a Liebig condenser arranged with just a slight slope down to the collecting vessel. When the liquid mixture is heated and vapors are produced, they enter the water cooled condenser and then flow down the tube, where they can be collected.

DISTILLED WATER: Water that has its dissolved solids removed by the process of distillation.

DOPING: Adding an impurity to the surface of a substance in order to change its properties.

DORMANT: A period of inactivity such as during winter, when plants stop growing.

DRAWING: The process in which a piece of metal is pulled over a former or through dies.

DRY-CLEANED: A method of cleaning fabrics with nonwater-based organic solvents such as carbon tetrachloride.

DUCTILE: Capable of being drawn out or hammered thin.

DYE: A colored substance that will stick to another substance so that both appear to be colored.

EARLY WOOD: The wood growth put on the spring of each year.

EARTHENWARE: Pottery that has not been fired to the point where some of the clay crystals begin to melt and fuse together and is thus slightly porous and coarser than stoneware or porcelain.

ELASTIC: The ability of an object to regain its original shape after it has been deformed.

ELASTIC CHANGE: To change shape elastically.

ELASTICITY: The property of a substance that causes it to return to its original shape after it has been deformed in some way.

ELASTIC LIMIT: The largest force that a material can stand before it changes shape permanently.

ELECTRODE: A conductor that forms one terminal of a cell.

ELECTROLYSIS: An electrical-chemical process that uses an electric current to cause the breakup of a compound and the movement of metal ions in a solution. It is commonly used in industry for purifying (refining) metals or for plating metal objects with a fine, even metal coat.

ELECTROLYTE: An ionic solution that conducts electricity.

ELECTROMAGNET: A temporary magnet that is produced when a current of electricity passes through a coil of wire.

ELECTRON: A tiny, negatively charged particle that is part of an atom. The flow of electrons through a solid material such as a wire produces an electric current.

ELEMENT: A substance that cannot be decomposed into simpler substances by chemical means, for example, silver and copper.

EMULSION: Tiny droplets of one substance dispersed in another.

EMULSION PAINT: A paint made of an emulsion that is water soluble (also called latex paint).

ENAMEL: A substance made of finely powdered glass colored with a metallic oxide and suspended in oil so that it can be applied with a brush. The enamel is then heated, the oil burns away, and the glass fuses. Also used colloquially to refer to certain kinds of resin-based paint that have extremely durable properties.

ENGINEERED WOOD PRODUCTS: Wood products such as plywood sheeting made from a combination of wood sheets, chips or sawdust, and resin.

EVAPORATION: The change of state of a liquid to a gas. Evaporation happens below the boiling point.

EXOTHERMIC REACTION: A chemical reaction that gives out heat.

EXTRUSION: To push a substance through an opening so as to change its shape.

FABRIC: A material made by weaving threads into a network, often just referred to as cloth.

FELTED: Wool that has been hammered in the presence of heat and moisture to change its texture and mat the fibers.

FERRITE: A magnetic substance made of ferric oxide combined with manganese, nickel, or zinc oxide.

FIBER: A long thread.

FILAMENT: (i) The coiled wire used inside a light bulb. It consists of a high-resistance metal such as tungsten that also has a high melting point. (ii) A continuous thread produced during the manufacture of fibers.

FILLER: A material introduced in order to give bulk to a substance. Fillers are used in making paper and also in the manufacture of paints and some adhesives.

FILTRATE: The liquid that has passed through a filter.

FLOOD: When rivers spill over their banks and cover the surrounding land with water.

FLUID: Able to flow either as a liquid or a gas.

FLUORESCENT: A substance that gives out visible light when struck by invisible waves, such as ultraviolet rays.

FLUX: A substance that lowers the melting temperature of another substance. Fluxes are use in glassmaking and in melting alloys. A flux is used, for example, with a solder.

FORMER: An object used to control the shape or size of a product being made, for example, glass.

FOAM: A material that is sufficiently gelatinous to be able to contain bubbles of gas. The gas bulks up the substances, making it behave as though it were semirigid.

FORGE: To hammer a piece of heated metal until it changes to the desired shape.

FRACTION: A group of similar components of a mixture. In the petroleum industry the light fractions of crude oil are those with the smallest molecules, while the medium and heavy fractions have larger molecules.

FRACTIONAL DISTILLATION: The separation of the components of a liquid mixture by heating them to their boiling points.

FREEZING POINT: The temperature at which a substance undergoes a phase change from a liquid to a solid. It is the same temperature as the melting point.

FRIT: Partly fused materials of which glass is made.

FROTH SEPARATION: A process in which air bubbles are blown through a suspension, causing a froth of bubbles to collect on the surface. The materials that are attracted to the bubbles can then be removed with the froth.

FURNACE: An enclosed fire designed to produce a very high degree of heat for melting glass or metal or for reheating objects so they can be further processed.

FUSING: The process of melting particles of a material so they form a continuous sheet or solid object. Enamel is bonded to the surface of glass this way. Powder-formed metal is also fused into a solid piece. Powder paints are fused to the surface by heating.

GALVANIZING: The application of a surface coating of zinc to iron or steel.

GAS: A form of matter in which the molecules take no definite shape and are free to move around to uniformly fill any vessel they are put in. A gas can easily be compressed into a much smaller volume.

GIANT MOLECULES: Molecules that have been formed by polymerization.

GLASS: A homogeneous, often transparent material with a random noncrystalline molecular structure. It is achieved by cooling a molten substance very rapidly so that it cannot crystallize.

GLASS CERAMIC: A ceramic that is not entirely crystalline.

GLASSY STATE: A solid in which the molecules are arranged randomly rather than being formed into crystals.

GLOBAL WARMING: The progressive increase in the average temperature of the Earth's atmosphere, most probably in large part due to burning fossil fuels.

GLUE: An adhesive made from boiled animal bones.

GOB: A piece of near-molten glass used by glass-blowers and in machines to make hollow glass vessels.

GRAIN: (i) The distinctive pattern of fibers in wood. (ii) Small particles of a solid, including a single crystal.

GRAPHITE: A form of the element carbon with a sheetlike structure.

GRAVITY: The attractive force produced because of the mass of an object.

GREENHOUSE EFFECT: An increase in the global air temperature as a result of heat released from burning fossil fuels being absorbed by carbon dioxide in the atmosphere.

GREENHOUSE GAS: Any of various gases that contribute to the greenhouse effect, such as carbon dioxide.

GROUNDWATER: Water that flows naturally through rocks as part of the water cycle.

GUM: Any natural adhesive of plant origin that consists of colloidal polysaccharide substances that are gelatinous when moist but harden on drying.

HARDWOOD: The wood from a nonconiferous tree.

HEARTWOOD: The old, hard, nonliving central wood of trees.

HEAT: The energy that is transferred when a substance is at a different temperature than that of its surroundings.

HEAT CAPACITY: The ratio of the heat supplied to a substance compared with the rise in temperature that is produced.

HOLOGRAM: A three-dimensional image reproduced from a split laser beam.

HYDRATION: The process of absorption of water by a substance. In some cases hydration makes a substance change color, but in all cases there is a change in volume.

HYDROCARBON: A compound in which only hydrogen and carbon atoms are present. Most fuels are hydrocarbons, for example, methane.

HYDROFLUORIC ACID: An extremely corrosive acid that attacks silicate minerals such as glass. It is used to etch decoration onto glass and also to produce some forms of polished surface.

HYDROGEN BOND: A type of attractive force that holds one molecule to another. It is one of the weaker forms of intermolecular attractive force.

HYDROLYSIS: A reversible process of decomposition of a substance in water.

HYDROPHILIC: Attracted to water.

HYDROPHOBIC: Repelled by water.

IMMISCIBLE: Will not mix with another substance, for example, oil and water.

IMPURITIES: Any substances that are found in small quantities, and that are not meant to be in the solution or mixture.

INCANDESCENT: Glowing with heat, for example, a tungsten filament in a light bulb.

INDUSTRIAL REVOLUTION: The time, which began in the 18th century and continued through into the 19th century, when materials began to be made with the use of power machines and mass production.

INERT: A material that does not react chemically.

INORGANIC: A substance that does not contain the element carbon (and usually hydrogen), for example, sodium chloride.

INSOLUBLE: A substance that will not dissolve, for example, gold in water.

INSULATOR: A material that does not conduct electricity.

ION: An atom or group of atoms that has gained or lost one or more electrons and so developed an electrical charge.

IONIC BONDING: The form of bonding that occurs between two ions when the ions have opposite charges, for example, sodium ions bond with chloride ions to make sodium chloride. Ionic bonds are strong except in the presence of a solvent.

IONIZE: To change into ions.

ISOTOPE: An atom that has the same number of protons in its nucleus, but that has a different mass, for example, carbon 12 and carbon 14.

KAOLINITE: A form of clay mineral found concentrated as china clay. It is the result of the decomposition of the mineral feldspar.

KILN: An oven used to heat materials. Kilns at quite low temperatures are used to dry wood and at higher temperatures to bake bricks and to fuse enamel onto the surfaces of other substances. They are a form of furnace.

KINETIC ENERGY: The energy due to movement. When a ball is thrown, it has kinetic energy.

KNOT: The changed pattern in rings in wood due to the former presence of a branch.

LAMINATE: An engineered wood product consisting of several wood layers bonded by a resin. Also applies to strips of paper stuck together with resins to make such things as "formica" worktops.

LATE WOOD: Wood produced during the summer part of the growing season.

LATENT HEAT: The amount of heat that is absorbed or released during the process of changing state between gas, liquid, or solid. For example, heat is absorbed when liquid changes to gas. Heat is given out again as the gas condenses back to a liquid.

LATEX: A general term for a colloidal suspension of rubber-type material in water. Originally for the milky white liquid emulsion found in the Para rubber tree, but also now any manufactured water emulsion containing synthetic rubber or plastic.

LATEX PAINT: A water emulsion of a synthetic rubber or plastic used as paint. *See* **EMULSION PAINT**

LATHE: A tool consisting of a rotating spindle and cutters that is designed to produce shaped objects that are symmetrical about the axis of rotation.

LATTICE: A regular geometric arrangement of objects in space.

LEHR: The oven used for annealing glassware. It is usually a very long tunnel through which glass passes on a conveyor belt.

LIGHTFAST: A colorant that does not fade when exposed to sunlight.

LIGNIN: A form of hard cellulose that forms the walls of cells.

LIQUID: A form of matter that has a fixed volume but no fixed shape.

LUMBER: Timber that has been dressed for use in building or carpentry and consists of planed planks.

MALLEABLE: Capable of being hammered or rolled into a new shape without fracturing due to brittleness.

MANOMETER: A device for measuring liquid or gas pressure.

MASS: The amount of matter in an object. In common use the word weight is used instead (incorrectly) to mean mass.

MATERIAL: Anything made of matter.

MATTED: Another word for felted. *See* **FELTED**

MATTER: Anything that has mass and takes up space.

MELT: The liquid glass produced when a batch of raw materials melts. Also used to describe molten metal.

MELTING POINT: The temperature at which a substance changes state from a solid phase to a liquid phase. It is the same as the freezing point.

METAL: A class of elements that is a good conductor of electricity and heat, has a metallic luster, is malleable and ductile, and is formed as cations held together by a sea of electrons. A metal may also be an alloy of these elements and carbon.

METAL FATIGUE: The gradual weakening of a metal by constant bending until a crack develops.

MINERAL: A solid substance made of just one element or compound, for example, calcite minerals contain only calcium carbonate.

MISCIBLE: Capable of being mixed.

MIXTURE: A material that can be separated into two or more substances using physical means, for example, air.

MOLD: A containing shape made of wood, metal, or sand into which molten glass or metal is poured. In metalworking it produces a casting. In glassmaking the glass is often blown rather than poured when making, for example, light bulbs.

MOLECULE: A group of two or more atoms held together by chemical bonds.

MONOMER: A small molecule and building block for larger chain molecules or polymers (mono means "one" and mer means "part").

MORDANT: A chemical that is attracted to a dye and also to the surface that is to be dyed.

MOSAIC: A decorated surface made from a large number of small colored pieces of glass, natural stone, or ceramic that are cemented together.

NATIVE METAL: A pure form of a metal not combined as a compound. Native metals are more common in nonreactive elements such as gold than reactive ones such as calcium.

NATURAL DYES: Dyes made from plants without any chemical alteration, for example, indigo.

NATURAL FIBERS: Fibers obtained from plants or animals, for example, flax and wool.

NEUTRON: A particle inside the nucleus of an atom that is neutral and has no charge.

NOBLE GASES: The members of group 8 of the periodic table of the elements: helium, neon, argon, krypton, xenon, radon. These gases are almost entirely unreactive.

NONMETAL: A brittle substance that does not conduct electricity, for example, sulfur or nitrogen.

OIL-BASED PAINTS: Paints that are not based on water as a vehicle. Traditional artists' oil paint uses linseed oil as a vehicle.

OPAQUE: A substance through which light cannot pass.

ORE: A rock containing enough of a useful substance to make mining it worthwhile, for example, bauxite, the ore of aluminum.

ORGANIC: A substance that contains carbon and usually hydrogen. The carbonates are usually excluded.

OXIDE: A compound that includes oxygen and one other element, for example, Cu_2O, copper oxide.

OXIDIZE, OXIDIZING AGENT: A reaction that occurs when a substance combines with oxygen or a reaction in which an atom, ion, or molecule loses electrons to another substance (and in this more general case does not have to take up oxygen).

OZONE: A form of oxygen whose molecules contain three atoms of oxygen. Ozone high in the atmosphere blocks harmful ultraviolet rays from the Sun, but at ground level it is an irritant gas when breathed in and so is regarded as a form of pollution. The ozone layer is the uppermost part of the stratosphere.

PAINT: A coating that has both decorative and protective properties, and that consists of a pigment suspended in a vehicle, or binder, made of a resin dissolved in a solvent. It dries to give a tough film.

PARTIAL PRESSURE: The pressure a gas in a mixture would exert if it alone occupied the flask. For example, oxygen makes up about a fifth of the atmosphere. Its partial pressure is therefore about a fifth of normal atmospheric pressure.

PASTE: A thick suspension of a solid in a liquid.

PATINA: A surface coating that develops on metals and protects them from further corrosion, for example, the green coating of copper carbonate that forms on copper statues.

PERIODIC TABLE: A chart organizing elements by atomic number and chemical properties into groups and periods.

PERMANENT HARDNESS: Hardness in the water that cannot be removed by boiling.

PETROCHEMICAL: Any of a large group of manufactured chemicals (not fuels) that come from petroleum and natural gas. It is usually taken to include similar products that can be made from coal and plants.

PETROLEUM: A natural mixture of a range of gases, liquids, and solids derived from the decomposed remains of animals and plants.

PHASE: A particular state of matter. A substance can exist as a solid, liquid, or gas and may change between these phases with the addition or removal of energy, usually in the form of heat.

PHOSPHOR: A material that glows when energized by ultraviolet or electron beams, such as in fluorescent tubes and cathode ray tubes.

PHOTOCHEMICAL SMOG: A mixture of tiny particles of dust and soot combined with a brown haze caused by the reaction of colorless nitric oxide from vehicle exhausts and oxygen of the air to form brown nitrogen dioxide.

PHOTOCHROMIC GLASSES: Glasses designed to change color with the intensity of light. They use the property that certain substances, for example, silver halide, can change color (and change chemically) in light. For example, when silver chromide is dispersed in the glass melt, sunlight decomposes the silver halide to release silver (and so darken the lens). But the halogen cannot escape; and when the light is removed, the halogen recombines with the silver to turn back to colorless silver halide.

PHOTOSYNTHESIS: The natural process that happens in green plants whereby the energy from light is used to help turn gases, water, and minerals into tissue and energy.

PIEZOELECTRICS: Materials that produce electric currents when they are deformed, or vice versa.

PIGMENT: Insoluble particles of coloring material.

PITH: The central strand of spongy tissue found in the stems of most plants.

PLASTIC: Material—a carbon-based substance consisting of long chains or networks (polymers) of simple molecules. The word plastic is commonly used only for synthetic polymers. Property—a material is plastic if it can be made to change shape easily and then remain in this new shape (contrast with elasticity and brittleness).

PLASTIC CHANGE: A permanent change in shape that happens without breaking.

PLASTICIZER: A chemical added to rubbers and resins to make it easier for them to be deformed and molded. Plasticizers are also added to cement to make it more easily worked when used as a mortar.

PLATE GLASS: Rolled, ground, and polished sheet glass.

PLIABLE: Supple enough to be repeatedly bent without fracturing.

PLYWOOD: An engineered wood laminate consisting of sheets of wood bonded with resin. Each sheet of wood has the grain at right angles to the one above and below. This imparts stability to the product.

PNEUMATIC DEVICE: Any device that works with air pressure.

POLAR: Something that has a partial electric charge.

POLYAMIDES: A compound that contains more than one amide group, for example, nylon.

POLYMER: A compound that is made of long chains or branching networks by combining molecules called monomers as repeating units. Poly means "many," mer means "part."

PORCELAIN: A hard, fine-grained, and translucent white ceramic that is made of china clay and is fired to a high temperature. Varieties include china.

PORES: Spaces between particles that are small enough to hold water by capillary action, but large enough to allow water to enter.

POROUS: A material that has small cavities in it, known as pores. These pores may or may not be joined. As a result, porous materials may or may not allow a liquid or gas to pass through them. Popularly, porous is used to mean permeable, the kind of porosity in which the pores are joined, and liquids or gases can flow.

POROUS CERAMICS: Ceramics that have not been fired at temperatures high enough to cause the clays to fuse and so prevent the slow movement of water.

POTENTIAL ENERGY: Energy due to the position of an object. Water in a reservoir has potential energy because it is stored up, and when released, it moves down to a lower level.

POWDER COATING: The application of a pigment in powder form without the use of a solvent.

POWDER FORMING: A process of using a powder to fill a mold and then heating the powder to make it fuse into a solid.

PRECIPITATE: A solid substance formed as a result of a chemical reaction between two liquids or gases.

PRESSURE: The force per unit area measured in SI units in Pascals and also more generally in atmospheres.

PRIMARY COLORS: A set of colors from which all others can be made. In transmitted light they are red, blue, and green.

PROTEIN: Substances in plants and animals that include nitrogen.

PROTON: A positively charged particle in the nucleus of an atom that balances out the charge of the surrounding electrons.

QUENCH: To put into water in order to cool rapidly.

RADIATION: The transmission of energy from one body to another without any contribution from the intervening space. *Contrast with* **CONVECTION** and **CONDUCTION**

RADIOACTIVE: A substance that spontaneously emits energetic particles.

RARE EARTHS: Any of a group of metal oxides that are found widely throughout the Earth's rocks, but in low concentrations. They are mainly made up of the elements of the lanthanide series of the periodic table of the elements.

RAW MATERIAL: A substance that has not been prepared, but that has an intended use in manufacturing.

RAY: Narrow beam of light.

RAYON: An artificial fiber made from natural cellulose.

REACTION (CHEMICAL): The recombination of two substances using parts of each substance.

REACTIVE: A substance that easily reacts with many other substances.

RECYCLE: To take once used materials and make them available for reuse.

REDUCTION, REDUCING AGENT: The removal of oxygen from or the addition of hydrogen to a compound.

REFINING: Separating a mixture into the simpler substances of which it is made, especially petrochemical refining.

REFRACTION: The bending of a ray of light as it passes between substances of different refractive index (light-bending properties).

REFRACTORY: Relating to the use of a ceramic material, especially a brick, in high-temperature conditions of, for example, a furnace.

REFRIGERANT: A substance that, on changing between a liquid and a gas, can absorb large amounts of (latent) heat from its surroundings.

REGENERATED FIBERS: Fibers that have been dissolved in a solution and then recovered from the solution in a different form.

REINFORCED FIBER: A fiber that is mixed with a resin, for example, glass-reinforced fiber.

RESIN: A semisolid natural material that is made of plant secretions and often yellow-brown in color. Also synthetic materials with the same type of properties. Synthetic resins have taken over almost completely from natural resins and are available as thermoplastic resins and thermosetting resins.

RESPIRATION: The process of taking in oxygen and releasing carbon dioxide in animals and the reverse in plants.

RIVET: A small rod of metal that is inserted into two holes in metal sheets and then burred over at both ends in order to stick the sheets together.

ROCK: A naturally hard inorganic material composed of mineral particles or crystals.

ROLLING: The process in which metal is rolled into plates and bars.

ROSIN: A brittle form of resin used in varnishes.

RUST: The product of the corrosion of iron and steel in the presence of air and water.

SALT: Generally thought of as sodium chloride, common salt; however, more generally a salt is a compound involving a metal. There are therefore many "salts" in water in addition to sodium chloride.

SAPWOOD: The outer, living layers of the tree, which includes cells for the transportation of water and minerals between roots and leaves.

SATURATED: A state in which a liquid can hold no more of a substance dissolved in it.

SEALANTS: A material designed to stop water or other liquids from penetrating into a surface or between surfaces. Most sealants are adhesives.

SEMICONDUCTOR: A crystalline solid that has an electrical conductivity part way between a conductor and an insulator. This material can be altered by doping to control an electric current. Semiconductors are the basis of transistors, integrated circuits, and other modern electronic solid-state devices.

SEMIPERMEABLE MEMBRANE: A thin material that acts as a fine sieve or filter, allowing small molecules to pass, but holding back large molecules.

SEPARATING COLUMN: A tall glass tube containing a porous disk near the base and filled with a substance such as aluminum oxide that can absorb materials on its surface. When a mixture passes through the columns, fractions are retarded by differing amounts so that each fraction is washed through the column in sequence.

SEPARATING FUNNEL: A pear-shaped glass funnel designed to permit the separation of immiscible liquids by simply pouring off the more dense liquid from the bottom of the funnel, while leaving the less dense liquid in the funnel.

SHAKES: A defect in wood produced by the wood tissue separating, usually parallel to the rings.

SHEEN: A lustrous, shiny surface on a yarn. It is produced by the finishing process or may be a natural part of the yarn.

SHEET-METAL FORMING: The process of rolling out metal into sheet.

SILICA: Silicon dioxide, most commonly in the form of sand.

SILICA GLASS: Glass made exclusively of silica.

SINTER: The process of heating that makes grains of a ceramic or metal a solid mass before it becomes molten.

SIZE: A glue, varnish, resin, or similar very dilute adhesive sealant used to block up the pores in porous surfaces or, for example, plaster and paper. Once the size has dried, paint or other surface coatings can be applied without the coating sinking in.

SLAG: A mixture of substances that are waste products of a furnace. Most slag are mainly composed of silicates.

SMELTING: Roasting a substance in order to extract the metal contained in it.

SODA: A flux for glassmaking consisting of sodium carbonate.

SOFTWOOD: Wood obtained from a coniferous tree.

SOLID: A rigid form of matter that maintains its shape regardless of whether or not it is in a container.

SOLIDIFICATION: Changing from a liquid to a solid.

SOLUBILITY: The maximum amount of a substance that can be contained in a solvent.

SOLUBLE: Readily dissolvable in a solvent.

SOLUTION: A mixture of a liquid (the solvent) and at least one other substance of lesser abundance (the solute). Like all mixtures, solutions can be separated by physical means.

SOLVAY PROCESS: Modern method of manufacturing the industrial alkali sodium carbonate (soda ash).

SOLVENT: The main substance in a solution.

SPECTRUM: A progressive series arranged in order, for example, the range of colors that make up visible light as seen in a rainbow.

SPINNERET: A small metal nozzle perforated with many small holes through which a filament solution is forced. The filaments that emerge are solidified by cooling and the filaments twisted together to form a yarn.

SPINNING: The process of drawing out and twisting short fibers, for example, wool, and thus making a thread or yarn.

SPRING: A natural flow of water from the ground.

STABILIZER: A chemical that, when added to other chemicals, prevents further reactions. For example, in soda lime glass the lime acts as a stabilizer for the silica.

STAPLE: A short fiber that has to be twisted with other fibers (spun) in order to make a long thread or yarn.

STARCHES: One form of carbohydrate. Starches can be used to make adhesives.

STATE OF MATTER: The physical form of matter. There are three states of matter: liquid, solid, and gas.

STEAM: Water vapor at the boiling point of water.

STONEWARE: Nonwhite pottery that has been fired at a high temperature until some of the clay has fused, a state called vitrified. Vitrification makes the pottery impervious to water. It is used for general tableware, often for breakfast crockery.

STRAND: When a number of yarns are twisted together, they make a strand. Strands twisted together make a rope.

SUBSTANCE: A type of material including mixtures.

SULFIDE: A compound that is composed only of metal and sulfur atoms, for example, PbS, the mineral galena.

SUPERCONDUCTORS: Materials that will conduct electricity with virtually no resistance if they are cooled to temperatures close to absolute zero (–273°C).

SURFACE TENSION: The force that operates on the surface of a liquid, and that makes it act as though it were covered with an invisible elastic film.

SURFACTANT: A substance that acts on a surface, such as a detergent.

SUSPENDED, SUSPENSION: Tiny particles in a liquid or a gas that do not settle out with time.

SYNTHETIC: Something that does not occur naturally but has to be manufactured. Synthetics are often produced from materials that do not occur in nature, for example, from petrochemicals. (i) Dye—a synthetic dye is made from petrochemicals, as opposed to natural dyes that are made of extracts of plants. (ii) Fiber—synthetic is a subdivision of artificial. Although both polyester and rayon are artificial fibers, rayon is made from reconstituted natural cellulose fibers and so is not synthetic, while polyester is made from petrochemicals and so is a synthetic fiber.

TANNIN: A group of pale-yellow or light-brown substances derived from plants that are used in dyeing fabric and making ink. Tannins are soluble in water and produce dark-blue or dark-green solutions when added to iron compounds.

TARNISH: A coating that develops as a result of the reaction between a metal and the substances in the air. The most common form of tarnishing is a very thin transparent oxide coating, such as occurs on aluminum. Sulfur compounds in the air make silver tarnish black.

TEMPER: To moderate or to make stronger: used in the metal industry to describe softening hardened steel or cast iron by reheating at a lower temperature or to describe hardening steel by reheating and cooling in oil; or in the glass industry, to describe toughening glass by first heating it and then slowly cooling it.

TEMPORARILY HARD WATER: Hard water that contains dissolved substances that can be removed by boiling.

TENSILE (PULLING STRENGTH): The greatest lengthwise (pulling) stress a substance can bear without tearing apart.

TENSION: A state of being pulled. Compare to compression.

TERRA COTTA: Red earth-colored glazed or unglazed fired clay whose origins lie in the Mediterranean region of Europe.

THERMOPLASTIC: A plastic that will soften and can be molded repeatedly into different shapes. It will then set into the molded shape as it cools.

THERMOSET: A plastic that will set into a molded shape as it first cools, but that cannot be made soft again by reheating.

THREAD: A long length of filament, group of filaments twisted together, or a long length of short fibers that have been spun and twisted together into a continuous strand.

TIMBER: A general term for wood suitable for building or for carpentry and consisting of roughcut planks. *Compare to* **LUMBER**

TRANSITION METALS: Any of the group of metallic elements (for example, chromium and iron) that belong to the central part of the periodic table of the elements and whose oxides commonly occur in a variety of colors.

TRANSPARENT: Something that will readily let light through, for example, window glass. Compare to translucent, when only some light gets through but an image cannot be seen, for example, greaseproof paper.

TROPOSPHERE: The lower part of the atmosphere in which clouds form. In general, temperature decreases with height.

TRUNK: The main stem of a tree.

VACUUM: Something from which all air has been removed.

VAPOR: The gaseous phase of a substance that is a liquid or a solid at that temperature, for example, water vapor is the gaseous form of water.

VAPORIZE: To change from a liquid to a gas, or vapor.

VENEER: A thin sheet of highly decorative wood that is applied to cheap wood or engineered wood products to improve their appearance and value.

VINYL: Often used as a general name for plastic. Strictly, vinyls are polymers derived from ethylene by removal of one hydrogen atom, for example, PVC, polyvinylchloride.

VISCOSE: A yellow-brown solution made by treating cellulose with alkali solution and carbon disulfide and used to make rayon.

VISCOUS, VISCOSITY: Sticky. Viscosity is a measure of the resistance of a liquid to flow. The higher the viscosity—the more viscous it is—the less easily it will flow.

VITREOUS CHINA: A translucent form of china or porcelain.

VITRIFICATION: To heat until a substance changes into a glassy form and fuses together.

VOLATILE: Readily forms a gas. Some parts of a liquid mixture are often volatile, as is the case for crude oil. This allows them to be separated by distillation.

WATER CYCLE: The continual interchange of water between the oceans, the air, clouds, rain, rivers, ice sheets, soil, and rocks.

WATER VAPOR: The gaseous form of water.

WAVELENGTH: The distance between adjacent crests on a wave. Shorter wavelengths have smaller distances between crests than longer wavelengths.

WAX: Substances of animal, plant, mineral, or synthetic origin that are similar to fats but are less greasy and harder. They form hard films that can be polished.

WEAVING: A way of making a fabric by passing two sets of yarns through one another at right angles to make a kind of tight meshed net with no spaces between the yarns.

WELDING: Technique used for joining metal pieces through intense localized heat. Welding often involves the use of a joining metal such as a rod of steel used to attach steel pieces (arc welding).

WETTING: In adhesive spreading, a term that refers to the complete coverage of an adhesive over a surface.

WETTING AGENT: A substance that is able to cover a surface completely with a film of liquid. It is a substance with a very low surface tension.

WHITE GLASS: Also known as milk glass, it is an opaque white glass that was originally made in Venice and meant to look like porcelain.

WROUGHT IRON: A form of iron that is relatively soft and can be bent without breaking. It contains less than 0.1% carbon.

YARN: A strand of fibers twisted together and used to make textiles.

Set Index